T0367264

Me

Skyara Reign

BALBOA.
PRESS

A DIVISION OF HAY HOUSE

Copyright © 2017 Skyara Reign.

All rights reserved. No part of this book may be used or reproduced by any means, graphic, electronic, or mechanical, including photocopying, recording, taping or by any information storage retrieval system without the written permission of the author except in the case of brief quotations embodied in critical articles and reviews.

This book is a work of non-fiction. Unless otherwise noted, the author and the publisher make no explicit guarantees as to the accuracy of the information contained in this book and in some cases, names of people and places have been altered to protect their privacy.

Scripture quotations marked NKJV are taken from the New King James Version. Copyright © 1982 by Thomas Nelson, Inc. Used by permission. All rights reserved.

Balboa Press books may be ordered through booksellers or by contacting:

Balboa Press
A Division of Hay House
1663 Liberty Drive
Bloomington, IN 47403
www.balboapress.com.au
1 (877) 407-4847

Because of the dynamic nature of the Internet, any web addresses or links contained in this book may have changed since publication and may no longer be valid. The views expressed in this work are solely those of the author and do not necessarily reflect the views of the publisher, and the publisher hereby disclaims any responsibility for them.

The author of this book does not dispense medical advice or prescribe the use of any technique as a form of treatment for physical, emotional, or medical problems without the advice of a physician, either directly or indirectly. The intent of the author is only to offer information of a general nature to help you in your quest for emotional and spiritual well-being. In the event you use any of the information in this book for yourself, which is your constitutional right, the author and the publisher assume no responsibility for your actions.

Any people depicted in stock imagery provided by Thinkstock are models, and such images are being used for illustrative purposes only.
Certain stock imagery © Thinkstock.

Print information available on the last page.

ISBN: 978-1-5043-0692-8 (sc)
ISBN: 978-1-5043-0691-1 (e)

Balboa Press rev. date: 02/17/2017

"I have seen much … I have seen love and I have seen horror. I have left this earth twice only to return with the memory of eternity. I am a woman, and I am gay. I am a seeker of truth and divine love. I am all of these things and yet none of them. My experiences and sexuality do not define me, for my identity, like yours, will always be safe, in love."

DEDICATION

THIS BOOK IS dedicated to all those who have taken their lives because the world around them didn't accept them.

This book is dedicated to all those struggling with their sexuality and their beliefs in God.

This book is dedicated to all those affected by homophobia.

CONTENTS

PREFACE

I WROTE *ME* as a beacon of hope to those struggling with their beliefs on sexuality and those who are struggling with their own sexuality.

I sat down for a coffee with a preacher who came out late in his career. Of course, not able to preach anymore, he shared his story and became a counsellor. After discussing his book, he encouraged me to tell my story because many of his clients struggling with sexuality and religious beliefs were women. He encouraged me to "write it for them."

It is my hope that readers struggling with their own sexuality find peace in knowing that they are a blessing from God and not a mistake. For those struggling to accept those who are different from themselves, it is my hope that in reading this book, you will see those different from you through the eyes of God.

ACKNOWLEDGEMENTS

I FIRSTLY WANT to thank God; without your presence since the day I was born, I would not be here, and I would not have survived. All the times I could have lost my faith, I never lost it in you. Thank you for creating me this way, and thank you for continually showing me why I am here.

I want to thank my mum, my dad, and my sisters for loving me as I am. This book and all I do is for you. I love you with all my heart.

I want to thank Simone Louise and my spiritual friends/tribe I have accumulated since my awakening. Daniela and Zara, Aleni and Chris, Melissa, Diane, Josephine Sartor, Vivienne Somers, Sue Edmonds, Jenny Blake, Frank Brancatisano, Kelly Rigby, and Rosemary Dawson. You all have been a part of my growth and journey. Thank you for sharing your light with me.

I want to thank my best friend, Daniela, who has always loved me for who I am and supports me in all my endeavours.

I want to thank my enormous family for always showering me with love and support. First cousins and second cousins, aunties and uncles, let's never stop being this ridiculously close. I love you all.

To all my friends, you are the family I have chosen, and I love you all immensely.

ACKNOWLEDGEMENTS

INTRODUCTION

God, make me a channel of your peace.

Where there is hatred, let me sow love;
Where there is injury, pardon;
Where there is doubt, faith;
Where there is despair, hope;
Where there is darkness, light;
Where there is sadness, joy.

Let the words that have exited my heart and landed on this paper bring abundant peace to those who are living in fear of who they are; there is a place and purpose on this earth for them too.

As I was driving, I was stopped by a vision of my grandmother. In shock, I missed the turnoff, and had I kept heading straight, I would have ended up at the burial ground where my grandmother resides. As I drove through the windy lane leading to my grandmother's grave, I remembered how much I love her. l felt her presence so strongly. I parked and slowly got out of the car, not knowing what I was experiencing. I walked over to her grave, and tears rolled down my cheeks; oh, how I missed her.

Suddenly, I heard a whisper that sounded a lot like her voice: "Look at the date of my birth and the date of my death."

Born on the eleventh day and died on the eleventh day. I did that to connect with you now, so you would know that I am always with you. I have never left. The idea that life and the other are on parallel planes, not so much different places, all of a sudden made sense. She is still living, just not on this earth plane.

"I want to show you something" she said.

I suddenly felt transported to a small town in the south of Italy. I knew instinctively it was my grandmother's town. I walked through the fields and saw the mountains of her town. I walked around and saw snow-covered streets and small farmhouses. I remember smelling the air; it was the freshest I had ever breathed in. It was so pure it hurt my lungs.

"I brought you here so that you could see where you come from. In my time, we fought to survive the day. Our goals, our dreams, and our ambitions were to survive the winter or get home from school in the freezing cold. Now in your time, you have endless possibilities and opportunities. The world is at your fingertips."

As she handed me a large gift that resembled a treasure chest of sorts, almost too heavy to carry, she said, "Just remember that when you achieve and succeed in your lifetime, you are doing it for all of us too; we are so proud of you."

I looked behind her as she spoke those words and saw my entire family, and they filled the mountain. There were too many to see, like an enormous army who all had faces that looked similar to mine. They were my family from generation to generation. I came to, kneeling at the grave of my grandmother and crying tears of mixed emotions, but mainly of joy. I knew I had a destiny that was worth fulfilling. I knew right then that I was here, as I am, for a special purpose that only I could bring to fruition. It is a very profound experience to really understand that the entire world is your family, and your entire family is the world.

A Meeting with Destiny

IT WAS AN ordinary morning; the alarm went off at five o'clock, but as usual, I was already awake, thinking about the day ahead of me and how to best execute the tasks. I ran a small café and was responsible for opening the doors. The earlier I got there, the earlier my regulars could stop in, hoping for a quick chat (or a lengthy talk) about life in general, their love lives, their kids, their husbands or wives, their failures and successes, and their hopes and dreams. I love that. I can't imagine what it would be like to be a therapist or counsellor; this felt somewhat similar, only without the professionalism or confidentiality, as we relied on good old-fashioned trust and friendship. Our conversations had no real boundaries; we would chat about anything and everything. I would watch as they took sips of coffee I had just made, and in that moment, I would instinctively know whether I had made it just right for them. I don't know why, but this brought me a lot of joy.

Sometimes, I would join them by having a piccolo myself, and we would share a moment or two. The taste of the coffee always provided an interlude to our conversation, changing the topic to discuss whether it was nutty or naturally sweet or bitter and so on.

Some of the descriptions I received about coffee over the years were quite amusing, such as, "Ahhh, this is liquid gold," or "Ahhh, my bitter-sweet addiction."

Most of the time, people expressed their love for this delectable drink; I was proud that I served them something they loved so much. One of my regulars, Zandra, came in this particular morning. As she waved her arms in the air and called out a prolonged "Good morning," I thanked God the coffee machine didn't have to heat up, as we used it so much, I rarely turned it off.

"Good morning," I replied, and we began a philosophical conversation that was typical for Zandra and me. We spoke mainly about God and the universe, synchronicity, destiny, and so on. Our conversations were deep. That's just how she was; she intrigued me. I grew up a devout Catholic, knowing Christians my entire life, so her new-age approach always got me thinking. I am open to God and even the new-age concept of a benevolent and intelligent universe. I always suspected that organised religion got it wrong somehow. It drove my mother nuts that her third daughter questioned God and religion from the day she could speak.

Zandra fascinated me with her approach to life, love, and the universe. I could chat with her for hours on end. We became such close friends that she would follow me around the kitchen sometimes, lending a hand, but mostly picking at the food I was cooking. Sometimes, she would throw a concept my way that blew my beliefs out of the water, and I would think about it for days on end. I loved and cherished these times with Zandra.

One morning, she came in with a paper about an enlightened lady who was coming into town to give a talk, and in the usual encouraging Zandra fashion, she suggested I go with her to the event. It was one of those things where you're happy for people to talk about their beliefs until the moment they ask you to go to church, and honestly, that's how I felt. I was thinking that there was no way I wanted to join a cult or follow some guru. I didn't want to have to pretend to be space travelling in meditations while actually praying for it to be over before I fell asleep. I was interested in knowing more about God and the universe, but I had given up on the idea that particular people or groups knew the way. I grew up in organised religion and witnessed nothing but corruption: Catholic priests molesting young boys (some of whom were my friends in primary school), money laundering ("hand over all your money, and God will make you rich" mentalities), and the list goes on. I have met many important priests, bishops, and ministers, as my mother is a devout member of the church. Many of them believe in healing yet are sick, believe in compassion yet are unforgiving, and believe in community yet kick people they don't approve of out of church.

Yes, church has failed me; I was spiritually bruised from a very young age. I saw through the eyes of a child who wanted to believe in unconditional love and strongly desired to possess immense mountain-moving faith, but I couldn't find it where it was said to be found.

I took the folded paper and reluctantly opened it up. After reading the date, I grinned and said I couldn't make it, as it was my mum's birthday on that day. In typical Zandra manner, she expressed that it mustn't have been meant to be: "If the universe wanted you to be there, it would have made a way."

We had had many discussions about synchronicity and how the universe conspired to make things happen. I had gone on with my day and forgotten altogether about the event. Days had past; I hadn't thought twice about it, but on one particular day, I had finished lunch service, and a customer was explaining a situation to me and had said repeatedly that he was just "keeping it real."

He said it so many times, I thought to myself, *Okay, buddy, I get it, you're keeping it real.* I didn't know why the phrase was playing on my mind when I sat down in the car that afternoon to go home, but the piece of paper Zandra had given me about the event was on the front seat; I was awestruck to find that the event was called

"Keeping It Real." I could hear the *Twilight Zone* music in my mind and thought, *Okay, that's a bit odd*, but brushed it off as a coincidence and drove home.

The event was now a week away; Zandra had made several appearances that week, never mentioning the event but continuing our conversations about the universe. I had finished serving coffees during another busy morning. While I was helping our barista with coffees, my wrist had cramped up. My mobile rung, and it was my mother. She said that we would have to celebrate her birthday on another day because she and my father had an event to go to. My parents, who never really go anywhere and always leave Sundays for family, were suddenly busy. How odd. I decided that it must have been a sign and so decided to go to the event Zandra had invited me to and get enlightened.

I had pictured the lady as a small Indian woman with a monk's robe and a dot in the middle of her forehead. Don't ask me why, but it's the image that came into my head when words like "enlightened one" and "guru" had been used to describe her. Most preacher types are men, so I also felt it interesting and intriguing that she was a woman. I suppose this was, in a way, my faith reactivating a little, especially considering I had received a few universal nudges and had decided to listen to them. I had suffered at the hands of the church in many respects, and so this was a huge step for me. I felt conflicted initially for deciding to go, but I had an emptiness inside that I was trying to fill, and I was hungry for something I couldn't put my finger on: maybe acceptance, maybe a spiritual guide. I'm not sure exactly where the longing came from, but by saying yes to this event, I felt like I took a step closer to answering my life's questions.

The day finally arrived. I made my way to the entrance and walked inside; at the top of the stairs, I came upon a woman who I thought was part of the audience. She looked at me intensely, as though scanning my soul; I wanted to react and pull away, but I felt weak. She pulled me in for a hug, and I felt as though I had lost all strength. An unusual electricity ran through my spine. The thought crossed my mind that she may be a witch and was doing some black magic, but there was something about her that felt safe.

Yep, this was the woman who was giving the discourse, and for the record, she didn't look at all as I had imagined. She wore trendy ripped blue jeans and a white tee. No dot on her forehead to be found. I walked away slowly, not knowing what had just happened, and took my seat ever so quietly. She began her talk, and I was glued to her for the next six hours.

I couldn't believe what I was hearing. She spoke about life and love in a way that was new to me. She spoke about the universe and how it works in a way I had never heard. She spoke about life experiences, past lives, and other concepts I did not know about. The thing is, for the first time in my entire life, everything made sense; *my* life made sense. I understood things about myself that I hadn't explored before; I saw myself in a different light and from a totally new perspective.

The life-changing part of the event for me personally was when she discussed the subject of sexuality. It was the first time I had heard a spiritual teacher say that homosexuality and uniqueness were a blessing. Those words blew my mind and forced my heart wide open. For the first time in my existence, I loved who I was, who I am. I realised I was not sick, like I had been made to believe my entire life, and in this realisation, there was no longer an overwhelming pressure to change.

Thinking about it now, as I am writing this, I still receive the feelings of unconditional love that I felt from her to me and from me to myself. Waves of love and acceptance flowed from her to me almost as though she was telepathically teaching me how to love myself. I was just silent during the intermission, pondering everything that had been said; she approached me and put her hand on my shoulder and quietly asked if I was okay.

I responded, "Yes, I think so. I'm just processing."

To which she replied, "It can be overwhelming … becoming aware."

Aware of what? I thought to myself, and then I realised that she was talking about being alive and being present. She has a saying that is "Where are you? Here. And what time is it? Now."

I had never seen faith in action; I had only ever heard it talked about, excluding the obvious spiritual leaders of the world. Before me stood a woman who didn't just speak about love and faith; she embodied it. I had witnessed so many Christians worrying more about being Christian than considering actually being like Christ, and yet here was this new-age-type woman who was so unreligious, making total sense about life and love.

The event came and went, but it was engraved in my heart and mind. I could not stop thinking about it all. It is important to mention here that prior to meeting this woman, I was in the middle of an extremely volatile and emotional period in my life. I would put on a smile and go to work, though I was no longer truly living, only existing, and had lost all hope about life and love. Spiritually wounded from my experiences with the church and church programs (which I'll discuss later on in this book), I was ready to give up. This woman was my hero. She had seen the darkness surrounding me and put out her hand for me to hold onto, showing me who I was in truth. She loved and accepted me for who I *truly* was. I will always love her for saving my life, and although I know she invoked what was already within, for that invocation, I am truly grateful.

A few months after the event, I remembered the woman saying she was available for private sessions. I felt the need to book one, as I had experienced such a huge awakening. I felt energised daily, to the point that I would wake up hyperactive after minimal sleep. I began to notice so many new things around me. I noticed my dreams a lot more. I noticed other people a lot more and took more time and care with them. I felt so alive and awake; I started taking care of myself. In fact, I lost sixty kilograms since attending the discourse, and it felt effortless. I lost a lot of weight, but I also noticed that there was no loose skin. For the amount of weight I lost, this was somewhat a miracle. I woke up wanting more out of life, but loving the here and now. Everything around me seemed more alive too, or maybe I was now simply present enough to notice the joy of being. I was revelling in this feeling of freedom, accepting who I really was in truth, and loving myself. I felt completely and utterly alive, knowing I could achieve anything. I felt strong and courageous.

Finding so much in this awakening, a part of me was lost as well. I didn't know how to process and make sense of the spiritual thirst that was still so new, and so I had a few private sessions with my new teacher. I didn't even know what this thirst was exactly. Meditation helped, and so I studied techniques and joined a meditation class. I learnt how to keep calm in a crazy world and how to connect and keep reconnecting to my true self, which I came to know as my higher self, the part of us that is, and always has been, connected to God. This higher vantage point taught me to embrace who I am with unconditional love and look at the world with eyes of unconditional love.

It was the beginning of my journey to self-actualisation.

Meeting this spiritual teacher reminded me of an event that took place six years earlier. I was in a relationship at the time, an abusive one, and the situation became so toxic that I had lost all hope and did not know what to do. My partner was abusive, and she would threaten that if I left, she would kill herself. I felt trapped, was alone, and didn't know how to deal with the situation. A friend of mine suggested I see the town psychic. This woman had a terrible reputation, and yet almost the entire town had seen her. I figured she mustn't be too bad if everyone goes to see her, and so I went. I went in the hope that she might tell me I had a bright future ahead and that if I left my girlfriend, she wouldn't kill herself. I hadn't come out at this stage and was very much in the closet. I had come out to myself but had never spoken about it with anyone, even my closest friends. It felt too hard, and I was afraid they wouldn't look at me the same.

I called and made the appointment. The woman seemed loving, kind, and welcoming. We greeted each other, and she invited me in to sit down and get comfortable. She immediately sensed the presence of my grandmother, and I immediately became emotional. She described how my grandmother lived and died, and she explained how my grandmother feels about me and my life journey.

I hadn't planned on mentioning I had a girlfriend and referred to her as my boyfriend for most of the session. Anxiety crept in as she accurately depicted my grandmother. *She is good at what she does and seems like the real deal,* I thought. I might be in trouble here.

The topic of relationships had come up, and I continued to refer to my partner as a male. The psychic kept saying that he had a very feminine energy, which I insisted on playing along with. The moment of truth came when she politely and very lovingly asked, "Sweetheart, is this person a woman?"

I cried in shame and for the life of me couldn't spit out the words. I was looking for words of explanation or words of reason, but I couldn't find any. She ever so gently said, "Oh honey, I don't care if you're gay or not. To me, you're human, and that is all."

I thanked her and told her that it meant a lot. I grew anxious and said that I hadn't told anyone and that I'd appreciate it if she didn't tell anyone either, as she knew the entire town, including most of the Italian community (she had married an Italian). She assured me that she would honour what was spoken about in the session, and she also went on to say that her gift was given to her to help people, not to destroy their lives. She also mentioned that I had gifts and I inherited them from my mother, who was a powerful closet psychic.

I laughed because my mother is a devout Catholic, and it just couldn't be, but one day, I asked my mother if it was if was true, and her response astonished me.

When I asked my mother if she had any spiritual gifts, she replied, "We all have them."

I then asked if she had specific gifts, like premonitions or being able to read into the future. She looked at me a little weird before telling me that when she was a child, she could see things others couldn't see, and she would sense when someone was going to die. She admitted to being able to read people well and know their intentions and what was in their hearts.

She used the words, "I could see the colours in their hearts and know about them." She finished by saying that it was a long time ago, and she asked for it to go away because it gave her anxiety and sometimes made her fearful.

The psychic also told me that I would split up with my abusive partner and that she would not go down without a fight. She also gave me some advice for what was to come in the following weeks.

After the session ended, she gave me a huge heartfelt hug and said, "Don't ever be afraid to be who you are."

I told her that I was terrified of being myself but thanked her and went on my way. The session got me thinking about life and love and being out of the closet. She was the first person I had told about my relationship with a woman. I couldn't even say the words "gay" or "lesbian" at this point. I felt a sense of relief by sharing my secret, and at the very least, I opened the closet door. Maybe it was just a toe outside the door, but it was something, and it took some weight off my shoulders.

A few weeks later, things were still rocky in my abusive relationship, and I felt consumed by it, again not knowing what to do. One particular Friday evening, when I had been so exhausted from fighting and carrying on with my girlfriend, I said the words, "God, help me end this," and went to sleep. It was a deep sleep, and I woke up at exactly 3:33 a.m. A vivid dream had woken me up, and I didn't know what to do, so without thinking, I called my best friend. By this stage, I had found the courage to tell this friend about my sexuality and my relationship. She said that she knew all along and was completely fine with my being gay. Coincidently, my friend was also awake at that time, which I thought odd after realising I had made the phone call so early in the morning.

She was worried and asked me to share the dream. In my dream, I had seen my girlfriend with the face of a rat, and she was sleeping with three other rats and a mouse. I continued to reveal that there had also been a voice describing the dream to me within the dream. The narrator explained that my girlfriend had been cheating on me with three other women and that they were depicted as rats because they knew she was in a relationship and didn't care. The mouse was innocent because she didn't know about the relationship.

During the dream, I had recognised who the mouse and two of the rats were, but I didn't recognise the third rat, so the narrator showed me a large Celtic tattoo on her back. My friend was at a loss for words; she was sorry I was going through this and told me that she would be there to support me. She also mentioned that she felt my partner seemed the type to cheat and had seen signs before but didn't know how to talk about it with me, as I hadn't told her about our relationship.

Not knowing what to do with the information I had just received, I decided to bite the bullet and confront my girlfriend. I also felt that her threat to kill herself was no longer a weight on my shoulders and that I would leave her once and for all. I had had enough. I would be sad if she hurt herself but would no longer carry the responsibility if she did; after all, it was her life and her decision.

I drove to her place, which was really meant to be "our" place, and as I drove past the entrance to the apartment block, I noticed her and another girl kissing as they entered the lift. In total shock, I suddenly remembering that I was driving and slammed on the brakes after almost going through a red light. I was angry, hurt, shocked, and relieved all at the same time. Finally, I had a solid reason for leaving (as though the three prior abusive years were not enough to call it quits).

I called her a few minutes later, and she answered in her normal fashion. I let loose on her while driving home. I told her what I had seen and told her about the others from my dream as well. She sounded totally in shock at the accuracy of my premonition, and I knew by the tone of her voice it was all true.

People have such a hard time telling the truth, even when they have been caught in a lie. I could never understand this. I have always been such a bad liar and lacked the detailed memory required to keep up with the lies. I have had many friends and lost many, all for the same reason: I have always been too honest. My mother always told me that my thoughts and feelings are always written all over my face. I now love this quality about myself because it helps me feel free and keeps my conscience clear. I guess by denying something about myself for so long, I was able to see how lies took a terrible toll on my heart, mind, and spirit. A lie is never worth the truth it takes away.

I finally left this abusive relationship and felt free on so many levels. I was finally free of the toxicity, ready to move on with my life. I have learnt to be grateful for all experiences in my life, good and bad. This was a lesson in life's journey for me; it was an uncomfortable one, but I learnt so much from it, above all, the valuable lesson of self-worth. I learnt to forgive and let go, and I found out what I do *not* want in a relationship. I have learnt to cherish tough times and hardened people because as humans, we all hurt, and our level of hurt is different. In suffering, we inflict pain on each other until we learn to love through pain and hardship. I truly believe all lessons lead us to the greatest lesson of life, which is unconditional love.

The woman who spoke at the event that day explained that we live in either fear or unconditional love, and the journey of life is forever guiding us to move towards unconditional love. I have chosen to keep pursuing love, no matter what happens. I will no longer allow perceived hardships and struggle to plunge me into fear, weakening me with its fragile insecurities and distorted judgements. Love will be my guide.

CHAPTER 2

My Upbringing

COMING FROM A devout Catholic Italian family, I was brought up in a quite traditional way. My grandparents lived with us, and we were one very big and happy family. My parents, born in Italy, migrated when my mum was in her teens and my dad in his early twenties. Both had very different reasons for migrating to Australia, but they shared the goal of creating a better life for themselves and their children. I considered myself so blessed growing up in my big, beautiful Italian family. My grandparents were my best friends; Nonna on my mum's side would tell me stories of what it was like living back in Italy in the mountainous countryside where she was from and how she would walk my mum to school in the snow. She would tell stories of how it was a hard time, and they didn't have much, but they loved each other deeply because life was more fragile back then; people valued life more because they understood on a very deep level that we could be here one day and gone the next.

She explained how they lived humbly and that times were not like now, where we have limitless possibilities and need not worry about survival. She would reflect on the times my nonno went off to war, and she wasn't sure if she would ever see him again. She told me that

that's why my mum was an only child, because he went off to war and didn't come back for a long time. My nonna on my dad's side would tell me stories of war and how there were times they would have to hide because bombs were being dropped. Till this day, I remember a story she would tell vividly about how she and my nonno helped an entire village of people hide in an underground train station; my nonno would go out on his little boat late at night to try and catch fish to feed everyone.

This part of the story is where Nonno would usually interrupt and say that he was out one night fishing for food when he was shot in the shoulder, the bullet still inside his chest. I could sit and listen to their stories all day long. I am close to all of my family and cherish our relationships. I would play Italian cards with my nonno, but he would hardly ever speak, as he was a quiet man. He said the war changed him, and he no longer had much to talk about, but when he would speak, his words were always profound. I always wondered what he was thinking as we played cards. What was going through his mind? Was he happy or sad?

I never could figure it out, but I do know that he loved his granddaughters more than anything in this world. For us, he would do anything, and we took advantage as much as we could by forcing him to participate in our childish games and wheel us around in a wheelbarrow. Whatever it was, he just couldn't say no, and we loved him for it.

My mother is known as the saint of the family. There was no one she wouldn't help. Volunteering at church, feeding the poor, praying with people who were dying or sick in hospital or helping family members get along better. This was my mum, and the entire family love her. My mother is in many ways my inspiration. I wish my heart was as big as hers. Her capacity to love people is admirable and a little like her dad; she couldn't say no. She was a giver, and people love her deeply. She was also quite open-minded. Before my sisters and I were born, she decided to move out of the overly Italian community where they lived after migrating to Australia and move to a suburb, where we would be forced to mingle more with Australians. In early primary school, we got teased for being wogs; it was sometimes hard to make friends, but my mother had the right idea. It wasn't long before the Australians were enjoying our culture and food, and we would enjoy theirs. After all, her children were born in Australia, and so she wanted us to be a part of its evolving multiculture. I struggled to understand this when I was a kid, but as I grew older, I appreciated her reasons while still cherishing our Italian culture. I have many fond memories of waking up on a Sunday morning to my grandmother making fresh homemade bread. She would teach me how to make it from scratch: how to prepare it, knead it, and let it rise. She would tell me how her mother taught her. Cooking was a daily part of our lives; I have so many incredible memories of tomato day, when we would make the tomato sauce, preserve it, and store it away, usually enough to last a year. I remember making preserves of olives, eggplants, artichokes, and giardiniera with my grandmother. They were beautiful days of cooking and preparation, along with interesting conversations and storytelling. Conversations many times would consist of heavy discussions on how women should behave and how we should grow and what we should aspire to when we are older. A must was getting married and having children, always behaving like a lady and maintaining a good reputation. The Italian culture is big on caring about what people think, mainly because of the communities they grew up in back in Italy. They would all know each other and all gossip about one another and what their kids were getting up to. I think part of Mum moving away from the community was because she didn't really believe in all that.

It's clear that the Italian culture was a huge part of my upbringing. We were as much Italian as we were Australian, and we were okay with that. I learned early on to love and embrace both, and both have served me well. There are a lot of things I love about the Italian culture, apart from the cuisine. I love how obsessively we love each other; I always felt wanted and loved by my family.

The stereotypes of Italians are usually true. They suggest that we are all about family and community and that we all live in the same street or neighbourhood. This was true for us. My aunty lived across the road, and cousins lived around the corner; we had to be near each other. I remember my aunty crying when I moved to Sydney and my parents trying to be strong and not let on that they had been crying. Sydney was only an hour away, but to them, it may as well have been the other side of the world. There isn't a day that goes by that they don't check on me and see how I'm doing or simply just want to hear my voice.

The Sydney move was a progression. First, I politely and respectfully stated that it was time for me to move out of home. I was thirty-two years old and desperately wanted a life of my own. Sure, living at home had its benefits, such as living rent free, a lot of homemade Italian cooking, a constant flow of visitors, and of course an abundance of love. I was the youngest, and I think my parents took my leaving the hardest, but they knew I needed my independence. I had great jobs with healthy income, so there was no reason I couldn't live on my own. As much as I love my family, our lives were always inundated with people, and I looked forward to time alone to read a book, meditate, or just think quietly. I craved alone time and rarely got it, so I was excited to go out on my own. I told my parents I would look for a house to buy and move into. They reluctantly agreed. I could see that they were sad, but they also wanted me to be happy. I searched the real estate websites and newspapers, but none of the houses I saw had the right feel.

Months had gone by and I was frustrated, but my parents were happy. I decided to call my friends and cousins who were in real estate and ask for them to consider me if anything came up (I don't know why I hadn't thought of this idea before). A good friend of mine suggested I decide what I really want and let an agent know exactly what it was I was looking for, including budget, number of bedrooms, size of backyard, and so on.

I had never really thought about it, so I decided to make my list of specifications, also adding that I wanted the house to make me money. After I shared my list, I received a phone call from one of my agent friends. He said that he had a house that had just gone on the market and thought this was the one for me. I trusted him and went to see the place. When I arrived, I loved it. It was a fixer-upper but was at a great price, and I had enough in my budget for a small renovation. I purchased the home.

Renovating was a nightmare; I don't think I'd ever do it again. I think I'd rather pay a builder to do the whole thing. Six months later, it was completed, and I was ready to move in. The first day I slept there, I was so happy and felt incredibly accomplished. I owned my very own home. I was independent. I was free to be me and loved my new independent life.

After a year passed by, property boomed, and my house almost doubled in value. What do you know? My property was making me money, as requested in my list of specs (which were really affirmations). I decided it was time to make the big move to the city. Yes, I loved my house, but I knew that my country townhome was not for me. I needed to be in Sydney. I was an aspiring artist, designer, and chef, and it was time I was in an environment where I could grow; unfortunately, my hometown had limited resources. Sydney was a creative place to be, with art galleries everywhere and exhibitions of all kinds happening constantly. It has an incredible nightlife, and I'm not just talking about clubs. People went out for dinner to amazing places, and the vibe was active and exciting.

I put the intention out that I wanted to move to Sydney. Within weeks, I was there; it happened so quickly. I believe it happens like that when it's meant to be, when we are in tune with spirit guiding us to our next chapter of growth. I went to see an apartment for lease and happened to be early. The agent suggested a private viewing because

I was so early, and I happily agreed. The place was decent and in an amazing location. I was ready to sign up. She gave me the documents to fill out, and within a week, I received a call that the place was mine. I love how life sometimes makes things move once you've made a decision. I believed with all my heart that Sydney would be the start of my journey, my journey of freedom, my journey of love, and my journey of awakening.

At that time, I attended a book launch for a friend of mine. She was the town psychic where I grew up and had written a book about her life. I loved this woman; she was a sweetheart. I really felt for her because we have a similar issue in our lives. Our families don't accept us as we are, her being a psychic and myself a lesbian. At her book launch, she told the story of how in becoming a well-known psychic and using the gift God gave her, she lost her family. Actually, her family stopped speaking to her because she married a divorcee and decided to be a full-time psychic. As she told the story, the pain in her face was visible; you could hear it in her voice as she spoke about how her own mother that didn't speak to her for years, including walking past her in the street and not acknowledging her. One day, she received a phone call that her mother was dying, and in her state at the time, she had a spiritual experience. After so many years of not believing in her own daughter, she uttered the words on her deathbed "I believe in you."

I was in tears listening to her tell the story; I wanted to hug her and thank her for having the strength to persevere in her career as a psychic because she may have lost her family, but she has helped so many people with her gift. She is definitely one of my heroes.

After the book launch, I was chatting to my friend, and she kept asking if I was okay. My eyes were red, as I had cried a great deal. "I think so," I told her.

She wanted to know why I was so moved, and I explained that in many ways, it may be a realisation I might face: my family never speaking to me again. I love my family so much, and on the journey of being myself, I have tried to love them through the process of feeling judged. There have been many times I have heard negative things said about homosexuals, and I know very well how they feel about it. My mother on many occasions said it was a sickness. Those words would tear my heart open, but I decided that I would ignore every negative word or thought they had towards me and return to them with unconditional love. That's how I really felt about them anyway. I love them for exactly who they are. I may not like how they feel or what they think, but they are my family, and I was determined to prove to them that my love was strong enough to resist any blow.

So you might be wondering how my family felt about homosexuality, in particular their daughter being gay. In short, they didn't approve (and that's okay). My mother thought that it was a sickness; in fact, when I came out to her, she said words to the effect of, "I gave birth to a woman, and you're a woman, damn it."

My dad was silent about it and only ever once had an outburst; he used the word "fag" in Italian and almost immediately covered it up by kissing my forehead and telling me he loved me. My sister said she didn't want it around her children. Over time, she relented and said she just wanted to see me happy. I'm so glad I hung in there and showed love where there was fear. As the saying of Saint Francis goes, "Where there is hatred let me sow love." I had to let them deal with their feelings and process them; had I retaliated with hatred, we may not still be one big loving happy family.

Despite staying in a place of love, this process was often heartbreaking. I wanted them to see that I was still me, the me they have always loved. I remember what killed me the most was my mother looking at me differently, like I was doing something wrong or dirty. Out of all my siblings, I was the one who was probably most responsible and a bit of a "straighty." I didn't smoke or do drugs; I couldn't even drink much, and still to this day, I am the cheapest drunk I know. I was so sick as a child that doctors warned me against party drugs due to all the medications I had growing up. They said it would be risky and I could die of a heart attack, so I never tried them out of fear. I tried smoking a few times but couldn't get the hang of it and really didn't like the taste.

I was the family clown and daredevil, but when it came to serious matters, everyone knew they could count on me to be there and be the responsible one. I was the youngest but I felt like the eldest. I was the one picking my older sisters up from the club at 3 a.m. or later. I was always the designated driver; when it was my turn to drink, I always got so sick. If I went past drink number three, I would throw up. Yep, three drinks, and I'm wasted.

I recently read *The Diamond Cutter: The Buddha on Managing Your Business and Your Life*; I was so blown away by the principles. After reading it, I was really proud of my family. Mum and Dad raised us with the value of always doing right by others as well as always acting and working with integrity. Integrity is everything. I remember my mother stressing to us about there being no such thing as white lies and that we should treat one another as we would like to be treated. *The Diamond Cutter* is based on the ancient ways of life dictated by the Buddha. I found that so much of it talks about how everything happens for a reason, and in a sense, it is a deeper message on the law of attraction. In particular, I remember a story he tells about a millionaire who had trouble buying a new home and how it was directly related to the fact that he had not given a bed and shelter to a woman who needed it.

Although this seems an unusual example, it explained a lot in my life and stood out as an important lesson as I read this book. I couldn't stop thinking about this story. It made me think about what I had ever done that was unethical or unkind; even if it was a white lie or something that seemed insignificant, it may have been significant to the person on the receiving end. My parents and grandparents were great believers in being kind to one another, giving to one another, and showing each other grace and compassion. They tried to teach us to be this way too.

I struggled with this a lot as I got older. I used to feel lost because it seemed the kinder I was to people, the crueller people were towards me; the more generous I was to people, the more people would take from me; the more loving I was, the more I experienced being unloved. I remember one day feeling so upset and angry because I felt like I was living life with my arms open and people were waiting in a line to crush me. I went into isolation for a while and felt it best to lay low. I went to work and came home, and that was it. I would meditate and spend time with my family, but I just felt like being alone and having time-out. In a meditation, it occurred to me that I was giving and loving because I had received so much love, and therefore, I had love to give. Maybe these people I was meeting didn't give love because they had never received it, like I had, or they were probably just having a bad day.

Mother Theresa once said:

> People are often unreasonable, irrational, and self-centered. Forgive them anyway.
>
> If you are kind, people may accuse you of selfish, ulterior motives. Be kind anyway.
>
> If you are successful, you will win some unfaithful friends and some genuine enemies. Succeed anyway.
>
> If you are honest and sincere, people may deceive you. Be honest and sincere anyway.
>
> What you spend years creating, others could destroy overnight. Create anyway.
>
> If you find serenity and happiness, some may be jealous. Be happy anyway.

The good you do today will often be forgotten. Do good anyway.

Give the best you have, and it will never be enough. Give your best anyway.

In the final analysis, it is between you and God. It was never between you and them anyway.

I realised that it wasn't about them but was always about me, in the sense that I am responsible for what I do and what I seek to bring to this world. I am responsible for my contribution, and blaming someone else for my change of heart was a poor excuse. I made my own mantra whilst this was happening. I would say to myself, "People will make you want to change your heart; don't let them." People will often try and make you see things from their perspective; it's great to listen and learn from others, but it is vitally important that in listening, you filter what serves you and what doesn't.

A close friend of mine would always say to me that there is no such thing as good and bad, only one's perception of it. I must say this used to aggravate me with a passion, and I would get so mad at her for saying this. To a point, I understand this to be true, in that if practiced hard enough, we can find the peace and truth in every situation. I learnt this lesson at work. I had hit my midthirties and was looking for a job where I could use my skills and serve the community at the same time. I was no longer looking for big bucks; I was looking for a job that would be rewarding as well as pay me fairly. I ended up with the role of head chef at an aged care facility and soon realised how much I loved caring for these people. Food would bring so much joy into their lives, and I made sure I catered to their needs and went above and beyond for them. I had found a job that I loved.

I noticed after the first pay cheque that the amount I was being paid was incorrect. My manager kept saying she would fix it, but after two months, it still wasn't fixed. I stood my ground and told her that

I was entitled to a fair pay and that she needed to fix it immediately. I reported the incident to HR and so forth; they acknowledged her wrongdoing and set out to fix her mistake.

The very next day, I was called into the office by my manager and asked to leave because of my behaviour. Unbeknown to me, she had lied about me swearing and carrying on in an unethical manner and said that there were a number of witnesses. I went home, and HR informed me that an investigation would take place. I thought we lived in a country where you were innocent until proven guilty; I was treated like a criminal. I felt completely helpless. I wondered why this was happening to me; my heart was aching for the residents, who had grown to love me and my cooking. I wondered if they were being fed well and if they were being looked after.

The investigation took place, and they discovered that there was no evidence to support her allegations against me; in fact, the witnesses said that no such event even took place. I was in a predicament I had no idea how to deal with. I cried for days over it. I was so hurt by the fact that she said I was aggressive, when I didn't even fight her on a lie. I took it and went home. After crying and going for long walks, I realised that even in hard situations, we have the ability to show love, and maybe in circumstances like this, the seeming antagonists need love the most. It was hard to think this way because my mind wanted me to take her to court and get her fired, as that's what I felt she deserved.

My heart, however, was telling me to show love and compassion whilst standing my ground. Living from your heart space doesn't mean that you're a pushover and everyone can take advantage of you. It simply means that whilst others are dealing with the chaos of life and being consumed by anger, fear, and jealousy, you show your power through love and kindness. Like Gandhi took all those blows and chose not to fight back but to show love instead, in the hope that through love and compassion, they would learn of their wrongdoings on their own accord.

Easier said than done, but whilst she was trying to get me fired, I chose to hang in there and do my job, constantly searching for that place in my heart that could love her enough to facilitate growth. As it turned out, she was fired within three months of my return, which proves the point in the story about the diamond cutter: We reap what we sow. Tempted to rejoice at her misfortune, I remembered that according to the ancient Tibetan law, celebrating someone's misfortune is one of the highest acts of unkindness there is. Nothing good can come from feeling good about someone else's suffering. Instead, I went home that day, grateful for my job, and I prayed for her and sent her waves of unconditional love and blessings.

People say to be careful laughing on your way up, for you may meet with the people you laughed at on your way down.

I woke up from this dream and vision in my mind, only to be suspended again for something else I did not commit. I had envisioned my manager taken away in handcuffs and fired because I felt someone like her did not belong in a nursing home. This, however, did not happen, and so I had to really think long and hard about what I was going to do in retaliation. I decided to resign, and in my report, I wrote as much as I could remember on the abuse I had witnessed and my own treatment from this manager.

A day or two after I resigned, one of the resident's children called me, extremely upset, asking why I had left. When I explained why, she pleaded with me to stay, saying I had a moral obligation to these elderly people to fight. She told me that her mother wanted to die; she no longer wanted to live in the nursing home. My heart bled for her and her mother; however, in my own heart, I knew that life is about balance, and some fights cannot be won alone. Was it my responsibility to fight for all those people, or was it the government's job to listen to my account of what took place and do something about it?

In my life, I have learnt how and when to fight; some battles are not meant for you. I stood up and fought as much as I could for the people at the nursing home, but I couldn't fight the entire fight, not on my own. I took a deep breath and remembered that it is not my job to save everyone. We must all truly save ourselves.

What an amazing world we would live in if we offered each other a helping hand when we were down and out, if we supported each other in the chaos of life and loved each other through our hardships. Sometimes, I think we forget that we truly are all brothers and sisters in this life, and we should treat each other as such. Despite my awareness of our unity, this experience at work was one of the hardest lessons I have ever learnt. Why is it so difficult for us to love someone who doesn't love us back? Why is it so difficult to show compassion to someone who seeks to harm us? It is because we have mistaken their behaviour for their identity. Their behaviour is just behaviour and could never change the truth of who they are.

We lose sight of each other once we start putting expectations on each other, entering this strange contract of love with conditions: I will love you as long as you behave, as I would have you behave. Everyone is divinely good at heart. All our poor choices simply reflect a feeling of lack, insecurity, loneliness, and fear. Let us give love freely so that these feelings of littleness disappear to reveal the love that we all truly are. Life comes and goes in the blink of an eye, as we all either desperately scramble for fleeting pleasures or peacefully dedicate ourselves to meaningful, selfless love. By failing to love my brothers and sisters, I am failing myself. By failing to love, we are failing each other, for love is what we all deserve. It is difficult at times, but we must break the cycle of judgement and negativity towards others, realising that we are all just as confused as the next person in our collective search for divine love. I want to close this chapter with the words my mother always said to me growing up: "There is room on this earth for everyone; always show kindness, and always be loving, and always treat people the way you would like to be treated."

CHAPTER 3

Surviving Sexual Abuse

THERE WERE MANY times as a child when I felt that I wasn't meant to be here. Something, many things, seemed fixed on my destruction since my arrival on this planet. When my mother was pregnant with me, she almost died and almost lost me too, but we both survived. Whilst pregnant with me, she injured her leg and burst a vein; she lost so much blood that she was rushed to hospital. We were lucky to be alive. I was born a few months later, and everyone was grateful I survived the ordeal; however, I was quite ill as a baby. I was very sick; doctors couldn't pinpoint what was wrong with me, so they pumped me with several types of drugs whilst trying to figure it all out. Shortly after, I got salmonella poisoning; doctors couldn't figure out how or why and concluded that it may have been due to all the mixed medications. Nevertheless, I survived that too. My mother says that I had had trouble breathing since she could remember, and when I was two, it was discovered I had chronic asthma. From then on until age thirteen, I was in and out of hospital every three to four weeks with several attacks. There were times my breathing capacity was so low, I would pass out.

When I was three, there was a mulberry tree in the backyard of our house that was right up against the fence of our property; the neighbours, my sisters, and I so loved playing in this tree, myself in particular. I loved to climb things. In fact, there was one time I climbed the house and got up on the roof, and I remember my grandmother and mother screaming for me to get down. I couldn't understand their panic back then; it was only a two-story house. One particular day, I had climbed the tree and was eating a few mulberries and leaning back onto a branch, enjoying them immensely, when the old man next door approached. It was a day that changed my life forever.

He knew I loved animals, and it began by me jumping down into his yard and playing with his dog, a beautiful German shepherd. He slowly lured me into the house for a few brief moments, as he knew when my mum would come out and check on me. He was calculated and knew how much time he had and the right moments to take me into the house and make it look like I had never left the yard.

The first time it he sexually abused me, I seemed to age instantly, burdened by the horrors of man's darkest expressions. It was like I had grown up and knew things far beyond my years and my comprehension. It was a sickening moment; I remember feeling exposed to the garbage of life, the depths of life's despair. I was one of five girls who were raped; I remember specifically lying on his dirty carpet floor, thinking that earth was a horrible place to be. I wanted to go back to where I had come from. I saw a darkness to life I didn't like and wondered why I was here and why this was happening to me.

As terrible as this may sound, I know now that this horrible experience was actually a blessing. I had the most profound experience with God whilst being abused. The abuse continued until I was six years old. I always felt as though God was protecting me and giving me strength to endure what was happening. It sounds crazy, but it's true. I had many moments with God, as my soul wandered off to amazing places whilst a terrible thing was happening in the physical. Sexual abuse is suffered by many; in fact, the statistics show that one in every three children experience sexual abuse (that are recorded). I maintain that I am blessed. I went through a horrific experience, yes; however, unlike the other girls who were attacked by the same man, I had a loving family who showered me with love and helped me through it as best as they could. As I mentioned, I was one of five girls who were attacked by the same man. The girls often looked scared, but I didn't have that fear. In fact, I felt that at times, I was taking one for the team and would tell him to let them go home because they cried and carried on.

Sometimes, he made us touch each other; this was my first-ever same-sex experience. There are so many subjects I'd like to touch on here; I will try and express them as clearly as I can. Sexual abuse did not make me gay. Being forced to perform acts with another girl did not make me gay. This dark chapter in my life was obviously a life lesson I needed to experience, but it has very little to do with my sexuality. At six years old, I had been raped by my next-door neighbour, once again feeling numb and zoning out as I had made a habit of doing in his presence, feeling a little lost.

I said to God, "Why don't you take me? I want to come with you, it's so amazing where you are."

I remember feeling that life was really shit, and I just wanted him to take me away to the paradise that I had experienced with him on several occasions. I closed my eyes, and all I remember this particular day is waking up at home. It felt like I closed my eyes in one place, and when I opened them, I was in another. Like magic. I remember this day clearly; coincidently, the day I said this particular "prayer" was the very same day one of the other victims grew the courage to tell her parents what had been happening.

Apparently, she couldn't contain the secret anymore and told her parents the truth. As I looked out the window, police cars had arrived at his house. It was over. I was hoping it would go away, but there was a knock at the door; yep, she told the police about me too. It was an interesting experience, as I had my first counselling session right there and then; the lady grabbed my Cabbage Patch doll (which I loved) and told me to point to where he had "touched me." I was fine to direct my hand near my doll's pelvic area, and then the lady asked if I would show her what he would do in that area. I remember feeling mortified that she would ask such a thing. I didn't want to do bad things to my doll; I was feeling so overwhelmed because I didn't really know what was happening or the extent of how bad it was. I didn't understand. Six-year-olds aren't supposed to understand sex; all I understood at the time was that I was being told something bad had happened to me, but no one would explain it. I was overwhelmed by a huge wave of emotions; my mind was a whirlwind of confusion. They tell me that what's been happening is really bad and that he is going to be punished for what he has done, and in my mind, I'm thinking, *This has been happening for a long time.*

Mum and Dad didn't know how to deal with it, either; I saw both my parents fall apart. Their baby was hurt. Dad and Mum suffered greatly, and I could see and feel their suffering. I wanted them to know that I was okay, to try and make it better for them, but it didn't seem to work. Like many parents, they chose to sweep it under the carpet and move on and just shower me with love and affection, but they didn't do that until they made sure I was physically okay.

Mum had remembered a time I had run home bleeding from my privates, and I told her I fell on the bar of my bike, as well as the times I had developed urine infections, so she made sure that everything was right with me physically. It was a tough time, and to make matters worse, shortly after that, the man who committed this crime actually ended his life before he could be tried.

I don't know why, but I felt guilty. *Did he kill himself because of me?* I thought.

Time went on, and I kept having nightmares. For years, I slept in my parents' bed because I was so afraid, and I didn't even know what I was afraid of. I would sometimes wake up screaming. Mum and Dad would ask, "What is it?" I didn't know.

I was so full of fear, and the asthma had only gotten worse. There were times I couldn't breathe and would wake up blue in the face for lack of oxygen. Mum and Dad were scared to let me sleep alone as well. There was one time I recall attempting to get out of bed to yell for Mum and Dad, but I couldn't because I couldn't breathe. I passed out at the door of my bedroom. Luckily, they heard the noise and rushed me to hospital.

I feel very grateful in seeing all this as a blessing, grateful for God's saving grace, and grateful that these events didn't ruin me. I wish my friends, the other girls who were attacked, had been so lucky. My heart bleeds for them. We experienced hell together and have a special bond. In my heart, I feel so deeply sorry that they didn't have the support I had and that they suffered far greater than I could have imagined. One of the girls, we will call her Maree, had a drug-addicted mother who died of an overdose when Maree was four. Her father was then sent to jail for possession, and she was raised by her uncles, who were in worse situations than her parents. She pretty much lived at my house, and my mum would feed her and buy her clothes. Mum tried to help her as much as she could, until she was seven years old, when she was sent to live with her grandmother on a farm. She kept in touch most of our lives, and my heart would bleed for her as she would tell me how her life would go from bad to worse. From age seven, I would send her clothes, money, and anything else she needed. I continued this until we were adults. There were periods where she went missing and wouldn't contact me for months. I would worry about how she was and if she was even alive.

Another of the girls, we will call her Sophie, was unable to cope with what had happened to her and fell into a depression at the age of six. Her family fell apart after the events that took place had come out. That's what happens sometimes; things like this destroy everyone's life, not just the victims, but also the people around them. Rumour has it that the parents both blamed each other for what had happened; it caused them to split. The split meant that the kids got separated from their father. The mother downgraded their house; they sold and moved to another part of town. I never saw Sophie again until our teens; by that stage, she was into drugs, and everyone knew her to be trouble. I tried talking to her a couple of times and told her that if she ever needed to talk, I'd be there for her, but she hated me. She hated that I still had my family, and hers had fallen apart. Later on in life, I found out that she had become a prostitute and was selling drugs in a town nearby.

Another one of the girls, we will call her Julie, was an only child; her parents also had a hard time dealing with what had happened. I didn't see Julie a lot after the event, as her parents rarely let her out of the house to play. We went to the same primary school, and I noticed she had become a loner, very quiet and rarely spoke. When school was over, she went straight home, and there was no interaction at all. I don't think her parents wanted her to be my friend, hoping she would forget what had happened. I ran into her every now and then when we were older; she had gone to a different high school. I noticed that she had huge scars all over her body. She would hurt herself and was also part of the drug scene. I was so protected by my parents; they monitored everything in my life, and so I always wondered how and where they were able to get drugs at such a young age. My high school was run by nuns, so there was no drug taking there. People got expelled for smoking a cigarette, let alone drugs.

The fourth girl was actually a member the perpetrator's own family. After the incident had come out, she and her family left town. I don't know what happened to her, but rumours got out that she had severe problems growing up, as he had done worse things to her (thinking maybe he could get away with it more because she was family). He had to be more careful with us so as to not get caught.

As an adult and even in my teens, I tried to reach out to them all, with minimal luck; I suppose they wanted to forget. We all had our issues growing up and enduring such an ordeal. I often wonder why I had it more together than them, and I'm not sure that's entirely true.

I just remember that my father told me this story after all this had happened. He told me there was a time in his life where he felt lost and didn't know what to do. His father wanted him to pursue a more lucrative career, and he wanted to pursue his dream. He said that he grew the courage to tell his father (he was his father's favourite) that he had made up his mind and would follow his dream. He knew in his heart that this was the right thing to do.

His father, being disappointed, expressed his disappointment and wanted nothing to do with him … for a time. My father said that he was so heartbroken because his dad was his hero. He went for a long drive and watched the sunset, and he said that whilst he was watching the sunset, he felt God speak to him and show him that everything would be okay. My dad often told me stories like this, but this one inspired me to never give up and never lose hope. Dad went on to say that this was the best decision he ever made and that everything turned out the way it was supposed to. Dad instilled in me a spirit of resilience to never let anything affect me to the point that it ruins my life. He was teaching me about choices and personal responsibility. He made me believe I could beat anything, and so I was determined to never let this situation beat me. At six, I gained this resilience; it didn't matter what happened to me externally. I would not let it contaminate me internally.

As I got older, I spent a lot of time in hospital. Between the ages of three and thirteen, I was in and out of hospital once and sometimes twice a month. My asthma was so bad at times, I was monitored closely through the night. One time, I remember the doctor asked my parents if a large group of uni students could observe my condition. My parents asked me if I wanted to do it, and I agreed to it. I remember being wheeled into a large room at the hospital on my bed; a group of students, around thirty or forty of them, came up to me and listened to my breathing and looked at my symptoms whilst having an attack.

I felt good about myself; the doctor made me feel special and told me I was helping them research my condition so that they could better treat patients. Doctors also tried experimental drugs on me, like different types of steroids. I hated taking them, but they made the attacks go away a lot quicker. The side effects, however, sometimes lasted for weeks. I hated being sick; to me there was nothing worse. I wanted to run and play like the other kids, without passing out due to lack of oxygen.

On my thirteenth birthday, as usual, I had an attack because I was getting excited about seeing the family and getting loads of gifts. Excitement brought on attacks too. In fact, there are many photos of me in my dad's arms whilst cutting the cake because I had no strength to sit up; I was that tired from not breathing. They were awful times; it is a terrible feeling, not being able to breathe. Shortly after I cut the cake, I got so bad that my face was changed colour and my lips turned blue.

I looked around the room, with my eyes slightly rolling backwards, and could see family members with fear in their eyes. Mum and Dad knew I had to go to hospital; they could tell this was a severe attack. Off I went to hospital, and by the time I got there, I was zoning in and out of consciousness. The doctors told my parents that I may not make it through the night, as my breathing capacity had plummeted so low.

I remember this night so vividly because I had an American doctor who was trying to talk to me and make jokes to get a response. I can still hear the accent. I remember drifting out of my body and being elevated. It's a weird feeling, but I recall my spirit coming out of my body, and the heaviness of life stayed with my physical body, whilst almost immediately, I was plunged into a state of absolute bliss. Everything felt good, and I was so happy.

In this state, I was walking around with Jesus, and we were having a conversation. I'm not sure if it was heaven, but it looked a lot like earth, only fresher, cleaner, more vibrant, and more beautiful. The Bible talks about how we get a new body in heaven, but as far as I could see, my body was still the representation of a physical body.

It just wasn't in physical form; it wasn't even tangible. I was part of everything, and everything was part of me; that's what it felt like, but I guess for the purpose of understanding the conversation between Jesus and I, it took place similar to what it would if we were in the physical.

He said the following words to me: "From this day onward, you will not suffer from this anymore; fear is now removed from you."

I woke up in my body and felt as fresh as I'd ever felt, almost reborn. For the first time in a long time, I took a very deep breath, deeper than in my entire life. Doctors were shocked and amazed. Mum and Dad were grateful. I am now in my thirties and have not had one symptom of asthma since. Doctors called me a miracle. Studies now show that asthma and fear have a lot to do with each other; it would seem my dream experience foretold the future of medicine. Doctors had asked what had happened, and I told them the truth. They didn't understand and didn't know what to say but were adamant that it was a miracle I survived; they were reluctant to send me home, just in case. I knew I was healed, but like any spiritual experience, it takes the world and people around you some time to catch up.

In my early thirties, if I was going on a holiday or playing a sport, Mum still would ask me if I needed to take a Ventolin with me. I still tell her I haven't used a puff in years, nor have I needed it. In fact, the first thing I did after being healed was jump into sports of all kinds, especially soccer. I loved soccer. Mum and Dad were so scared, but after a few years of watching me running around without having to get rushed to hospital because I had collapsed, they got used to it and started to enjoy watching me play. I had my life back.

In my teens, I noticed that I wasn't the same as my sisters and my friends. I always knew I was different, but this was the age when having a boyfriend was important and going out with friends and meeting boys was the thing to do, especially if you wanted to be cool and fit in. All my friends started getting boyfriends, and many times at parties, my friends would try to set me up with a boy. I was never interested and tried to change the subject of dating. I had lots of male friends, and we got on as mates. I would chat to them about soccer and sports in general, occasionally about cars. We are all unique, and I believe I am just as much feminine as I am masculine; there are many things I love and enjoy about both qualities.

I met a guy and got along with him really well and decided to make him my boyfriend. Our relationship was more a friendship, but we really enjoyed each other's company, and I tried to get away with passing him as my boyfriend. Whenever he tried to kiss me or show affection, I tried to divert his attention, but being a young male, that was difficult. He wanted to "do stuff," and at times I let him. I remember hating it, and he knew I wasn't into it. We dated for almost a year, and the poor guy kept trying with me.

When we broke up, I figured I'd proven to everyone that I was straight and could now relax, finish school, and pretend I was heartbroken for a while and not ready to date again. Mind you, I went to an all-girls Catholic school run by nuns, so I could also get away with not dating because I was considered too young, or I could play the Catholic card. I did concentrate on school and eventually worked a part-time job after school. I never really thought about having a relationship because I couldn't, not publicly anyway, and being in the closet is so hard.

On my cousin's eighteenth birthday, she invited everyone to a house party, a party her parents didn't know about, as they were away. A friend of hers had a crush on me for some time, and she told me that we should start dating on the night of her party. I knew this guy and liked him a lot. He is a beautiful guy and was probably the best person for what unfolded to happen with. This guy was marriage material and wanted me as his wife; he had made his mind up. We did get together at my cousin's birthday, and he declared his feelings for me. He was such a beautiful guy, I agreed to date him, and we started a relationship.

After dating for a while, he knew something was wrong, and I told him that I wasn't ready for a relationship. He was a gentleman and said he would wait for me. I told him to move on with his life. Two years later, we happened to be invited to my cousin's engagement, and by this time, I was feeling a little lonely, I guess, and people were wondering why I was single, and so the opportunity came up, and he asked me out again. I said yes and really gave it a go.

I had overheard my sisters talking about a gay friend of ours; my sister asked him how he knew he was gay if he had never slept with a woman. I felt the answer was obvious: He didn't want to; that's how he knew he was gay. It got me thinking that when I came out to them, they would present me with the same argument, and so I slept with my boyfriend. The experience was okay in the respect that he was a wonderful lover and really took care, and I could tell he loved me a lot. I felt so guilty because he was making love to me, yet I didn't feel the same way. I didn't love him, not romantically.

A week went past, and I hardly spoke to him. He texted and called, but I didn't respond because I didn't know how I was going to break it to him that I didn't feel the same. I knew in my heart I needed to tell him because he had a right to be happy; he was such a beautiful soul. He deserved to be loved and honoured back. I couldn't be what he wanted or needed, and so I decided to let him go. It was wrong of me to make him feel like he was constantly doing something wrong, when all he was trying to do was love me. This was a valuable life lesson for me on love: Love must honour and serve both parties. I grew the courage and told him that it wasn't him, it was me, and that I didn't love him or want him the way he wanted me.

I was surprised that he was upset, but I believe he knew why. I just wasn't ready to tell anyone. He kissed me politely on the forehead and told me that he hoped I'd find what I was looking for, wishing me all the happiness in the world. Even to this day, when I see him, he still has so much love for me; he's a true gentleman and a wonderful person.

If he reads this book, I want him to know that I'm sorry and still grateful to have experienced such a wonderful friend, and I wish him a world of happiness. This situation taught me about connection and electricity, as well. Chemistry is a hard thing to master, but in a romantic relationship, it really is everything. When you know that there is an energetic pull that brings you together, and when you join forces, magic happens, and this feeling has never happened for me with a man. The chemistry just isn't there; it never has been, and I've accepted that. I've stopped trying to make that happen. In the words of Paolo Coelho, I'd prefer the universe to conspire to bring us together so that I can entertain the magic about to unfold.

I'd like to end this chapter by stating firmly once more that my sexuality was not determined by the incidents that happened when I was a child or my experiences later on in life. My sexuality is a blessing from God, and I am perfect just the way I am; nothing to change here. I believe I chose to come through and be born as a gay woman in this lifetime, and I believe that part of my purpose here on this earth is to demonstrate that love cannot fit in a box. Love is love. I know that many religious people reading this will not agree, and that's okay; you are entitled to believe as you wish.

I want you all to know that I love God, and I believe he loves me exactly as I am. He created me this way for a reason. Someone once told me I was here on earth to teach people nonjudgement on this issue. I'm not sure about that, but I know my purpose so far has been to accept and love God's creation as he created it. A great friend of mine once expressed to me that if her husband came through as a woman, she would be a lesbian because she knows she was meant to be with him in whatever form he came into. I believe there is a lot of truth in that. I also believe that beyond the labels and categorisations of identity, we are all human beings in search of love and with many different expressions of it, and that's okay. There is room enough on this earth for all of us.

CHAPTER 4

Growing Up in the Church

GROWING UP IN a devout Catholic family made for many family dinners with the local priest, church every Sunday (every day for my mother), and dedication to prayer and meditation on God's word. My earliest memories are my love for God. I didn't really understand who he was, but I loved him anyway. Loving him gave me peace. Loving God made a lot more sense than anything else, for me, anyway. Our church consisted of families who didn't believe in contraception; some had more than twelve children. I enjoyed Mass at times, not really with the traditions, but I enjoyed the life lessons taught in scripture; for some reason, I had the ability to really read into them. In my adult years, I studied the Bible quite a lot and came to the conclusion that God was trying to teach us to love each other, unconditionally. I feel that I understood this as a child too. I could feel the love in his words.

When I was thirteen, I had a near-death experience (NDE) and experienced God in a real and very personal way. I found that in the church I grew up in, I couldn't find the God I experienced during my NDE. I wanted more. I wanted something more tangible, and so I moved into Pentecostal-type churches, as God seemed to work through people there. I wanted to see and experience him in a real and personal way.

My first experience was great; the music was awesome, and they had real singers. The fantastic sermons were about relatable and relevant life lessons. Everything started to make more sense here. After I had been attending for several weeks, there was an altar call. If you wanted to accept Jesus into your heart and be a true Christian, you could accept Christ publicly and walk to the front of the church, where loving people would pray with you and for you to develop a life dedicated to Christ. That day, I accepted. I don't know why, but I felt I wanted to be part of this group of people who experienced the miracles of this tangible God. I didn't feel different saying yes publicly, as I felt I had already invited Christ into my heart, but nevertheless, it was nice to share the moment of surrender with others.

The next big step was to be baptised. I felt embarrassed and really didn't want to do it, but if it were for God, then I would do it. I would show my dedication, and my willingness to be immersed in water was a reflection of my willingness to be immersed in the Holy Spirit. I didn't feel any different. I still felt a little embarrassed. I didn't feel any closer to God; more importantly, I felt like I was participating in tradition, a bit like Holy Communion and Confirmation with the Catholics (and yes, I went through that too). I have had all the sacraments (and then some).

From this point, life went on, and I never let on about my sexuality, as I was enjoying Bible study and the sermons at church. Years went by, and I was now late into my teens; I had had several girl crushes and closeted relationships, and prayed to God daily to remove these desires, as they were not acceptable to the church. I played the game for as long as I could, until one day, I was at a family function and noticed that one of the girls in my Bible study was secretly dating my cousin. I wondered why she was keeping it a secret because Catholics were still Christian; I didn't understand why it mattered. After she was found out, she asked me not to say anything, and I respected her wishes.

Shortly after that, though, she convinced my cousin to change religions and become a "true Christian." He loved her enough that he decided to go through with it, as it seemed important to her. Now is a good time to mention that several of my cousins knew about my sexuality and embraced me as one of the boys, even though that wasn't really what I wanted; that's how they took it, so I went with it. They shared too much about their personal lives, including details of their sexual encounters (my newly confirmed cousin included). I knew that my Bible study friend wasn't a virgin, according to my cousin, and she was worried that I might say something and expose her (despite the fact that I instinctively knew her decision was not an issue in the eyes of God, only the church). To her, it seemed I had more information about her than she was comfortable with, and so she decided to tell my Bible study group of my sexuality.

To my surprise, I was asked to no longer attend. I agreed that it was best for the group and moved on. Feeling as hurt as I did at the time, I cried out to God in desperation for Him to cleanse me of this "illness." Despite being convinced that I had an illness, I was also convinced that my treatment and lack of support did not reflect Christian values. Looking back now, I can see that their behaviour didn't even reflect basic human ethics. I decided to move on to another Pentecostal church. In this church, I was a little more covert and decided to lay low and not tell anyone too much about myself. The first day I was there, the youth group leader approached me as I was leaving the service.

"Stay for coffee," she suggested.

I agreed, and as we began to chat, she said that the Holy Spirit told her that I was gay; she had made it her mission to help me through it and be healed. I was shocked and also a little excited that this girl seemed to know the answer to my life questions of why this happened to me and how I could be free of this "burden." I told her that I felt so bad that I had these feelings and desperately wanted them to go away. I wanted to be normal and feel like I could love a man and get married and so on.

She set out to help me; I'll never forget her words, as I cried tears of hope that she could help me be free of this. She said that "sin is sin, it doesn't matter what it is; it's all the same in the eyes of God. Your sins are no different than my sins; God sees them all as sins." She also said I needed to stay single until these feelings were dealt with; if I chose not to pursue an avenue of healing, I would not be accepted at church. I agreed to follow her instructions.

The first recommendation was a healing retreat to prepare myself for an "ex-gay ministry," which I was to attend later on. I was also put on a waiting list for Bible study because they didn't know where to put someone like me.

Church life was an interesting journey. The message of God is really about love and acceptance. The entire New Testament is based on the vision of one man. His vision was beautiful. He referred to our unity as the Sonship, teaching that unconditional love will lead us to the kingdom of heaven within. Christ loved *everyone*. I couldn't understand why God would heal me of asthma at thirteen and yet not heal me of this as well (if it needed fixing, that is). Church was supposed to be a place of love, and yet you would be politely informed of the reasons you were unlovable.

The level of hypocrisy blew my mind, as did the conditional love and also the lack of kindness. This part of my journey was probably the hardest. I felt so terribly alone and surrounded by people who wouldn't accept me if I didn't conform to who they wanted me to be. I was lost and had felt these feelings for so long that I truly didn't know if I could change enough to satisfy them. Once the discussions had begun about changing my sexuality, a part of who I am, I began to feel pressure but was determined that if there was a chance I could change, for the sake of my family, I would try it with all my heart and soul.

It would be wrong of me to say that God wasn't present in the churches I grew up in and the ones I migrated to. I still firmly believe that these sanctuaries are sacred and special, and I believe our reverence for God is reflected in their architecture and regal design. People often go to church because they are hungry; their soul is hungry for truth and direction. I believe that God is present, and church has its place in this world. Like my mum says, there is room enough on this earth for us all. The older I get and the more I seek God, the more I have discovered that if I take time to just be in the peace of God, I can tune in by watching a sunset or sunrise. I can tune in by stopping to notice my breath or feel the breeze on my skin. In the stillness of life, we can tap into our own soul; that is where God resides: in everything and a part of us all. That is my belief, anyway.

I was so moved when I read *The Alchemist* by Paolo Coelho and the discussion between Santiago and the desert. He speaks to the wind, the sun, and then the hand that wrote all, until finally, God is revealed to him. It is a reflection of himself. This scene in the book moved me to the point of tears. We are a reflection of God: part of this perfect love that created all. It has been said that there are two important days in our lives: the day we are born and the day we discover *why* we were born. Isn't this why we seek God: to find out why we are here and what it is we are meant to do? Church teaches many of life's lessons, and I am eternally grateful for the introduction to faith that I received from the Catholics and Pentecostals. Many of their teachings are beautiful and love based, and those are what I hold dear; others I am happy to let go of and move on.

Church life was an interesting one in many respects. Church was a way of life, not just attendance on Sundays. Church meant participating in all church activities and events for the purpose of growing the congregation and spreading the message of Jesus. It also meant hanging out with church folk; at times, I truly understood why people called it a cult. I remember feeling as though my church friends would refer to my family as if they were lost souls and evil, just because they remained Catholic. I remember being excused from activities as soon as someone found out about my sexuality or found out that I had a partner, which meant I was caving in to my desires. I volunteered in many things at church and gave a lot of my income and could be relied upon for tasks and events. It became evident to me that they were happy to take my money, my connections, and my skills, but they would never accept me (not whole-heartedly anyway).

I handled the food deliveries for the church café and often paid for the food, as a sign of my devotion. One afternoon, while attending to these duties, I had an altercation with one of the leaders at the church. This leader had become my friend and felt the need to speak to me about why my sexuality was such a grave sin. I responded by mentioning that Jesus spoke about a lot of things, yet the son of God, the most important figure in the Bible, never mentions anything about homosexuality. I had been studying theology and trying to work this out for myself, and I picked up on the fact that Jesus never mentions anything about homosexuality, and yet we are crucified at church.

He did, however, speak about divorce and how we love each other; this leader was divorced but was allowed all the privileges at church that I would be denied because I like women. I had so many questions; each time I would ask for some guidance or assistance in discovering the truth, I was considered rebellious and disrespectful. I was asked to leave and talked about in a negative way.

My goal is not to defame the church; I hold church dear to me still and occasionally enjoy a visit. I pray that those who seek growth through religion can look past the distortions that limit love, preventing us from seeing the grander vision that Christ could see. If you are experiencing judgement in a religious institution, I pray that God gives you the strength to forgive and show compassion, reminding those in positions of leadership that Christ's message was about love. For those in positions of leadership within the church, I pray that you call on Christ and the Holy Spirit to reveal the true nature of love to you. May the essence of Christ's teachings never be lost in politics, narrow ideologies, or limited perspectives. Christ's vision was beautiful. Do not trade its sunrise for a cloud.

I still held a great deal of anger towards the church; several years later, I went into a meditation and spent hours trying to make sense of it all whilst asking if God could take away these feelings of anger and resentment. In my meditation, I saw a beautiful sunrise and writing in the sky, saying "Today is a new day." I felt the message clearly in my heart. If I want them to love me for who I am, I need to love them for who they are, exactly as they are. I finally understood and felt completely at peace. I felt empowered and decided that I would always respond by giving love, regardless of what was given to me. It felt so good to stop fighting. The fight was one I couldn't win (not with anger in my heart, anyway).

I watched an old movie about Gandhi, and there was such a powerful line where Gandhi is in front of an audience in South Africa. He said, "We will fight but not with our fists. They will torture, attack, and imprison us, and we will take the blows, but we will not return them, for in our suffering, they will eventually see their wrongdoing."

This is obviously no comparison to that, but I too had many bruises, torture, and imprisonment. My wounds were spiritual, all because people struggle to love those who are different, whether it is the colour of their skin or their sexuality. Christ was really quite a revolutionary and a rebel. His "turn the other cheek" wisdom is the ultimate rebellion against violence and has inspired people like Gandhi to lead people out of oppression: not just political oppression, but the spiritual oppression we often see in the judgement and separation of religious organisations. If only we could look at the world through the eyes of our hearts, we would see each other through unconditional love. In the depths of us all, there is purity.

Gandhi said that we are all too imperfect to judge one another, and that is why I leave judgement up to God. There were many times I burnt with anguish at church, listening to sermons that told me I was unacceptable. My soul was crying out to be itself, the expression it chose to be upon entering this earth, constantly at odds with the world around me. It's an interesting experience, thinking and feeling as though you are sick or something is severely wrong with you, when in fact, it's just that people are uncomfortable with who you are.

It was hard to register that the issues were theirs and not mine. Church was meant to give me purpose, sanctuary, belonging, and peace. Instead, I was cast out and made to feel undeserving of the light that belongs to us all. When I first sat to write this book, my friend shared an article about a pastor who wrote a book about being kicked out of church after coming out. Intrigued by this man and his story, I messaged him directly on Facebook, and as it turned out, he lives ten minutes from my apartment. I received a message ten minutes later, and he suggested we meet for coffee. I was blown away by this man and his incredible story. He was a Christian pastor who had a congregation of ten thousand or more people, part of a huge international church organisation, and now author of a bestselling book, now he was sitting in a café with me, sharing church stories.

He said that he didn't really know what to do with himself after being kicked out of the church, and so he became an advocate and counsellor for people struggling with homosexuality, in particular Christians who were suffering. I told him about the book I planned to write, and he explained how vitally important it was and encouraged me to write it in a spirit of love: unconditional love for the people who would both learn from it and grow from it.

I felt inspired but overwhelmed; writing this meant that I would have to relive moments I wished to forget. I realised, though, that it would be healing and therapeutic to revisit past pains and sufferings, and look at them from the perspective of the grown woman I now am. I no longer felt those pains the same; it is true that time heals wounds, as deep as they may be. Without the contrasts in life, we couldn't evolve. With narrow perspectives comes the longing for a higher perspective, which brings me to one of my favourite scriptures in the Bible:

There is a time for everything, and a season for every activity under the heavens: a time to be born and a time to die, a time to plant and a time to uproot, a time to kill and a time to heal, a time to tear down and a time to build, a time to weep and a time to laugh, a time to mourn and a time to dance, a time to scatter stones and a time to gather them, a time to embrace and a time to refrain from embracing, a time to search and a time to give up, a time to keep and a time to throw away, a time to tear and a time to mend, a time to be silent and a time to speak, a time to love and a time to hate, a time for war and a time for peace (Ecclesiastes 3:1–8).

This scripture always reminds me that there is a purpose in the duality of everything we experience; life will always be beautiful if we choose to see it from a higher and more loving perspective. Easier said than done, I know, but life is a journey, and Rome wasn't built in a day. Besides, the journey itself is truly beautiful. In some ways, I feel as though we have already arrived. Time is irrelevant in heaven. No matter how long it seems we have struggled in time, the outcome for us all was always guaranteed in heaven, in eternity.

From this perspective, we don't have to take our lives so seriously. The little distortions and challenges become almost comical: like the church asking me to stop being gay. How is it was possible to stop being gay? I searched for an off switch when I took it seriously, but now I can laugh about it. A lot of my past frustrations with church were because they wanted me fixed immediately. This issue sparked the question of whether it was a choice or not. Was I choosing this?

This question took me to a space of deep self-discovery. I searched my memories for the first time I felt attracted to women. From as far back as I can remember, I knew who I was and never actually had an issue with it, until I realised how my family, some friends, and my church felt about it. I grew up with older sisters and watched how they behaved over boys, and I knew I was different from them. I didn't feel the same. When I was older, I knew why there was silence when I would say that I loved a certain actress or singer or how I wanted to be with them. As a child, I expressed my love for a female singer, and as soon as I was old enough, I wrote her a passionate love letter and wanted my mother to post it. I begged her so much that she finally agreed to post it, just to shut me up. Like most parents, maybe, she thought I was going through a phase and hoped it would go away. To this day, I truly believe that my parents love me unconditionally for who I am and as I am. I feel that their behaviour was motivated by fear: fear of my navigation through life and the judgements and hardships I could face. Who could not love their parents for this kind of love? They just wanted to protect me.

I will finish this chapter with a story about a lion and lioness that were travelling with their cubs. The parents were killed in a terrible accident, and the cubs were taken away. One of the cubs managed to escape but found himself in the jungle all by himself. As he wandered around, he came across a flock of sheep and decided to hang around with them. As he grew, he learned from the sheep and behaved like the sheep and soon began to think like a sheep. As a full-grown lion, he still believed he was a sheep and travelled around with his fellow sheep, baaing just like them. Suddenly, the flock was attacked by a group of lions; they killed most of his fellow sheep, leaving him untouched. One of the lions approached him and said, "Why are you baaing? You're a lion, not a sheep."

He said, "I am a sheep, and you killed my brothers and sisters."

The lion looked confused and said, "Here, eat some of the sheep."

The lion refused; however, as the other lion brought the flesh of the sheep closer to his face, he could smell the blood, and his instincts kicked in. In that moment, he forgot he was a sheep, and for the first time in many years, he let out a horrifying roar and ate the remains of the sheep.

The first time I heard this story, it broke me. As we journey through life, there are times when we will pretend to be someone we are not; we may even be convinced that we are this made-up character. Whatever the reason may be, whether we are being something to please others, pretending in order to fit in, or simply seeking love and acceptance and constructing a distorted idea of what that is in our own minds, whatever the story, we will always come back to our true nature. We will always have a moment in life when we look in the mirror and honestly see our true selves. This story taught me the importance of being my true self after many years of pretending to be straight in an effort to avoid being ostracised.

When I moved to Sydney, I lived near a strip of amazing restaurants and cafés. I would walk daily along this beautiful esplanade; one morning, I walked past a Brazilian restaurant. It was six o'clock in the morning, and I was finishing up my walk. Of course, the restaurant was closed, but there were some remains of celebratory items lying around on the floor, probably from the night before.

It reminded me of a night when a couple of church friends wanted to drive to Sydney from our hometown and enjoy an evening at one of the biggest church organisations in Australia. An international preacher was coming, and we didn't want to miss him. The plan was to enjoy the evening at church and then go to a café and have coffee and dessert. The church service was great, as I loved this preacher. He seemed genuine and really loving, and I loved hearing his sermons (I still do). Once the service was over, we couldn't decide where we wanted to go; there were so many choices.

"How about Samba Brazil?" one of the women suggested, and so we went there.

The food was great, and the company and conversation was great too. Within twenty minutes or so, a group of Brazilian dancers came out into the restaurant and started dancing. I have seen Brazilian shows before and thought nothing of it. The girls were stunning and had amazing physiques, and man, could they dance. They knew how to shake it, that's for sure.

I noticed that a couple of the women looked disgusted and gave some very strong judgemental looks to the Brazilian girls wearing barely anything and dancing. We finished our meals and coffees and decided it was time to head back.

In the car, someone said, with judgement, "Can you believe how naked they were and parading themselves around like that?"

I asked if they had ever seen a Brazilian show, explaining, "It's part of their culture to dance, and I personally think those costumes are amazing."

I was the only lesbian in the group, and I admired the detail that went into their costumes, but these straight Christian woman couldn't stop talking about their tits and arses. I found it amusing, anyway.

Noticing that I wasn't participating in their judgements, they said that it was no wonder that fate would have it that we would encounter such an experience; clearly, I must have attracted this kind of vulgarity, seeing this as a supposed temptation for me. They even suggested I needed prayer and deliverance from the event that had just occurred, due to the fact that I was still attracting this into my life (it had nothing to do with the fact that they performed there every weekend; there were signs everywhere stating that fact). Nope, I must have attracted the Brazilian dancers, which was the cause of us participating in such a vulgar and perverse event. It was all my fault.

After we got back home, within days, the entire church knew. I feel that we all must take a serious look at our ideas and beliefs, especially the ones that facilitate our growth. Unfortunately, most religious organisations have allowed distorted ideas to prevent the original essence of the teachings from being understood. All religions are about love, nonjudgement, unity, compassion, kindness, purification, personal growth, and growth within the broader community. As far as religions go, I truly feel that if there is ever a focus on anything that causes separation between people, then the teaching has certainly lost its essence.

CHAPTER 5

False Beliefs on Sexuality

SEXUALITY IS SO broad and complex that it cannot be easily categorised. It involves feelings and desires, and none of these can be described in one word. Many people might think it's a simple case of either "gay" or "straight," but sexuality is multifaceted. There are transgender, transvestite, lesbian, gay, bisexual, bigender, bicurious, asexual, cisgender, demisexual, drag queen, drag king, femme, fluid, female-to-male, male-to-female, transsexual, gynesexual/gynephilic, heterosexual, intersex, pansexual, two spirit, and more.

This book is not intended to be an academic discussion on labelling sexuality; I have chosen to focus on only a few issues I have personal experiences with: transgender, transvestite, gay, lesbian, transsexual, bisexual, and homosexual.

The following definitions are from *The Oxford English Dictionary* (2014):

> **Trans*/Transgender** – (adj) (1) An umbrella term covering a range of identities that transgress socially defined gender norms. Trans with an * is often used to indicate that you are referring to the larger group

nature of the term. (2) A person who lives as a member of a gender other than that expected based on sex assigned at birth.

Transvestite – (noun) A person who dresses as the binary opposite gender expression ("cross-dresses") for any one of many reasons, including relaxation, fun, and sexual gratification (often called a "cross-dresser," and should not be confused with transsexual).

Gay – (adj) (1) A term used to describe individuals who are primarily emotionally, physically, and/or sexually attracted to members of the same sex and/or gender. More commonly used when referring to males/men-identified people who are attracted to males/men-identified people, but can be applied to females/women-identified people as well. (2) An umbrella term used to refer to the queer community as a whole, or as an individual identity label for anyone who does not identify as heterosexual.

Lesbian – (noun) A term used to describe women attracted romantically, erotically, and/or emotionally to other women.

Transsexual – (noun & adj) A person who identifies psychologically as a gender/sex other than the one to which they were assigned at birth. Transsexuals often wish to transform their bodies hormonally and surgically to match their inner sense of gender/sex.

Bisexual – (adj) A person emotionally, physically, and/or sexually attracted to males/men and females/women. Other individuals may use this to indicate an attraction to individuals who identify outside of the gender binary as well and may use bisexual as a way to indicate an interest in more than one gender or sex (i.e., men and genderqueer people). This attraction does not have to be equally split or indicate a level of interest that is the same across the genders or sexes an individual may be attracted to.

Homosexual – (adj) A [medical] term used to describe a person primarily emotionally, physically, and/or sexually attracted to members of the same sex/gender. Is considered stigmatising due to its history as a category of mental illness and is discouraged for common use (use "gay" or "lesbian" instead).

Personally, I don't agree with labelling any meaningful part of the human condition, especially sexuality. It is too restrictive since the intention is to box, limit, and name an ineffable concept or idea.

When adults look at a tree, there is no childlike wonder or curiosity because we know it is simply a tree. We are not open to perceive the stability of its roots, the strength of its bow, its journey ever-reaching into the light, or its delicate leaves that thank the sun and share its life. Above all, we don't know how much this tree can teach us about ourselves, because it's "just a tree."

I was out one night with a group of friends at a local bar. It had already been a fun night when some friends of friends arrived. We got talking in the usual introductory ice-breakers of likes, dislikes, and occupations. I connected with one individual in particular; her name was Chanel. She was immaculately dressed, with an equal inner beauty. After exchanging stories for a while, I noticed she had an Adam's apple, as well as other masculine features, like large hands, a deep voice, and what looked a faint shadow of hair around her chin and neck. I didn't think twice about it as we continued speaking; I focused on her eyes and looked deeply into them. (A wise person once told me we should look into a person's eyes and see each other for the souls that we are, beyond what we see in the physical.)

Whilst looking into her eyes, I noticed that the energy I was feeling from her was so incredibly beautiful and transcended my ideas of gender, identity, and even the physical body. I hope I always see those before me with curious eyes and through a childlike heart, perceiving the wonder and splendor of their being. May I never need to define the infinite nature of being.

Over the years, I have experienced feminine women who like women, feminine men who like women, masculine women who like men, masculine men who like men, and so on. The reality is that we are all unique. One could argue that our values, ideas, and beliefs are shaped by our past experiences, but I don't believe this is valid for sexuality. What happened in my past didn't make me gay, straight, or bi.

While undergoing religious gay therapy, they really tried to push the idea of *imprinting*. I decided to read up on the subject and found there are many studies on its use for changing people's mind-sets.

Imprinting aims to determine the source of our ideas and beliefs and then looks at how, through practice, we can change the imprint and, therefore, ourselves. I agree that this can work in terms of our decision-making, but for me, sexuality is not (and never was) a decision. I was born this way. It may be easy for people who are straight to disagree with this sentiment, but they have never had their sexual preferences questioned, so how would they know what it feels like to be judged or ostracised for a natural feeling they have always had?

I have been searching my entire life and purposefully went to great lengths to change my so-called "programming." It never worked: not from praying, dating men, attending gay rehab, or wishing I was different. I am as I was born and as I am meant to be. I am over seeing myself as broken and in need of fixing. I am just me, as God (or the universe) made me. And a greater force than I made me a lesbian.

Now, I only seek to change my ideas of evolution, personal growth, and empowerment. Personally, I believe in the concept of reincarnation. This puts a whole new slant on the subject of sexuality. If you consider that we've experienced many lives in many different forms, including different genders, then it would be fair to say we have experienced many forms of sexuality also. You might be straight this lifetime, but who knows about the next? I would suggest sexuality is irrelevant to our spirituality. We are a soul, and this is without gender or sexual orientation.

Even if you look at the medical establishment, early psychiatrists differed on their views of homosexuality. Freud actually thought it was a natural variation of human sexuality, while others, such as Sandor Rado, argued that it was pathological. The pathological view prevailed, and the dominant theory became that homosexuality was the result of abnormal sexual development or even early childhood trauma and abuse. In the first half of the twentieth century, what little research was done supported the pathological hypothesis, but in retrospect, this research was highly biased.

In 1974, homosexuality was removed from the *DSM* as a mental disorder. Now, forty years later, this remains the robust conclusion of psychological research: Homosexuality is part of the healthy spectrum of human sexuality; there is no evidence that justifies the conclusion that it is a disorder or disease.

Judgement and separation seem to be a cyclical theme throughout the history of humanity. We begin with love, encounter things in life we don't really understand, and our fear of this causes us to segregate and discriminate until something happens to make us once again realise the beauty of uniqueness, and then we return to love again. Trans actress Laverne Cox once said something that I find so powerful: "All the things that make me uniquely and beautifully trans – my big hands, my big feet, my wide shoulders, my deep voice – are beautiful."

The population on this planet is ever growing, and the appreciation of uniqueness can only expand in this unprecedented time of instant information and communication. May we abandon the need to judge and label, and may we all enjoy our individuality while understanding that there is an element of unity and oneness in this. Through love and acceptance, we are all the same.

I will not conform to a label. Yes, I prefer women and am drawn to them romantically, but is it really necessary to categorise me? Who is helped by this? A friend once said, "If my husband came into this world a woman, I would still find him/her and be with him/her. The fact that this would label me a lesbian means nothing." This same friend also said that "when we look at one another, it would be beautiful if we saw the soul; then we would know all we need to know about the person."

I asked her how this was possible; she said that it was easy; we would only need to take the time to look into each other's eyes more and study each other more, not in judgement, but in love.

A great misconception of our era is that neuro-linguistic programming (NLP) has something to do with sexuality. I believe this is the reason being gay has been considered an illness for so long and also the reason for all the ministries and programs that were created to "change" sexuality.

An international program promoting gay rehab states the following on its website:

> Proclaiming that faith in Christ and a transformed life is possible for the homosexual through the transforming power of Jesus Christ. Equipping Christians and churches to uphold the Biblical view of sexuality but respond with compassion and grace to those affected by homosexuality. Serving people affected by homosexuality through Christian fellowship, discipleship, counselling, support groups and other services.

Please notice the words used, such as "affected," suggesting that homosexuality is an illness or disorder of some sort. For the record, I do not believe this to be true.

The NLP done in the ex-gay ministry I was a part of suggested that there were deep-rooted triggers that caused a person to swing a certain way (for lack of a better term). I have attended many seminars on the subject of neuro-linguistic programming and have also participated in many of the exercises. Although these programs were useful for changing bad habits, thought processes, and behavioural patterns, they did not (and could not) change my sexuality.

I have met several people from the church community who argued this point with me; our conversations led me to a very interesting discovery: Many Christians confuse same-sex attraction with other completely different tendencies and do not allow space for the necessary distinction between a natural tendency and one created through conditioning and circumstance. One woman told me that she had been a drug addict and in a same-sex relationship with her cousin. She was trying to explain to me how our stories were similar; she left the gay world and entered a Christian life, where she could be straight.

I explained that incest is a very different from a same-sex couple; I didn't understand her issue, as I had never thought about sleeping with family. This woman was proud of her story and used it to help others who struggled with homosexuality. For me, it did not make sense. I struggled to understand how homosexuality was her main issue. She had come out of a same-sex relationship with her cousin, married a preacher, had three children, and lived happily ever after. I am happy for her, if she is truly happy, and I do not criticise her story; we all have one, and they vary in so many ways. Since meeting this woman, I have met several like her who are adamant that they are no longer lesbians. I intend on being transparent in this book, and so I wish to state that many of these women are still struggling. Some have truly found their way, others have gone "back" to being lesbians, and others have chosen to remain celibate and single. All of these life changes can be positive, only if they have brought them happiness and fulfilment, though I do not see how fulfilment could be found by supressing and denying our inherent tendencies. It is like putting a Band-Aid on a deep wound. If it is not treated it, will fester and cause serious problems in the future. How can you grow as an individual without acknowledging and understanding your own desires?

Another serious false belief within the church is the inability to distinguish same-sex attraction with paedophilia. I have heard many preachers compare homosexuality with paedophilia and other crimes, often expressing that they are one and the same. At the healing ministry I attended, they would say things like, "You do realise it is one and the same? They are all perversions."

This was extremely upsetting for me to hear, as I had experienced sexual abuse first-hand as a child. These words would haunt me; for many years, I would have nightmares about being caught sleeping with a woman. I would ask them how this was possible, seeing that homosexuality was not a crime. I would also ask how they could compare these things when one form of sex was consensual, between two adults wanting to love each other, and the other was not consensual; it was also illegal.

When I would ask such questions, they would say I was being rebellious and would then work on rebuking and exorcising my rebellious spirit. Although writing this book has been cathartic and liberating at times, there have been many moments when I have had to stop to release tears of pain and anguish as I relive the hurtful ignorance in these experiences. I survived all of this for a reason and hope that my story could save someone. If there is pain in my story, may it be there so that people who have experienced the same do not feel alone in their anguish, and if there is joy, may it be there so they can rejoice in the freedom and peace that is coming.

Our individual path to happiness is truly unique; eventually, the labels we insist on will cease when we realise that we are all on the same journey, walking upon infinite and diverse roads that all lead to the same place: self-actualisation. This is not just a new-age concept but a scientific one also. Evolution cannot be restricted to biological phenomena alone. Our evolution clearly takes place on an intellectual, emotional, and spiritual level, as well. We are all so unique, and yet in this evolution of self, we are one in our journey to happiness.

In my research for this chapter and how sexuality and beliefs go together, especially regarding the church, there is another false belief that I must mention here: Gay men were encouraged to start a relationship with a gay woman; it was strongly believed by the congregation that this "solution" would help. I experienced this distorted therapy first-hand. I call this the "two gays together make a right." There were several other gay men and women, mostly men, who were visibly picked as being possible homosexuals. Part of the purpose of me writing this book comes from many moments when I looked around the church and witnessed teenage kids I knew were gay; my heart bled for them. I feared for their journey ahead and prayed that they would not suffer persecution as I did and not run away from God, either. Some of them had parents heavily involved in the church, and I feared the condemnation that would come from the congregation towards the individuals and their families. It's funny that the people I got along with most at church were the people who also suffered persecution due to being divorced or of a different nationality; even widows felt the harshness of judgement from the church.

Sometimes, it's as though church paints a picture of the perfect family, with the perfect house, and if people don't fit into this type of picture, they quickly become second-class citizens. I was friends with several divorced women and a widow, and they treated me with love and acceptance because they so desperately wanted that from the church. The widow was one of the most beautiful people I have ever met; she not only was a widow (losing her husband to cancer), she also had a severely disabled son. She often told me the church made her feel as though she had brought this all upon herself.

The church often used the book of Job as an example of how the law of attraction attracted this into her life; she was in some way paying for her sins, past or present. She felt such a lack of compassion from the church, and I witnessed her crying many nights, falling asleep to a bottle of wine. I say she is beautiful because despite how the church treated her, she still loved people so much that she forgave them every day; she blessed them and thanked Jesus for the compassion He has for her every day. I felt bad at times crying to her about my problems; I had joined her Bible study because I wasn't allowed to be in a younger women's Bible study for fear I may try and sleep with them all. I felt bad telling her my anguish with the church because she was going through so much herself, but she would always pray for me. One evening, she asked me to stay back once everyone had gone home, and she spent some time praying over me. I will never forget this night or the words she prayed over me; they went somewhat like this:

"God, look after this beautiful girl, send your army of angels to protect her from the attacks of people, fill her heart with your love so that she has the capacity to love them despite their actions. I ask that you anoint her with the spirit of King David, that like him she would seek your heart in everything that goes on in her life, and like David, give her the intelligence to fight the Goliath in her life. Don't let her fight with her hands or the toxicity that may exit her mouth; instead, teach her to fight as David did with your wisdom and your accuracy and your love, always seeking to do what is right. May she also always know that she is loved and accepted always by you. Keep her and bless her always on her journey, in Jesus' name I pray."

I thanked her and went home. This prayer moved me because she knew I would have to fight the church for my right to be there and to be accepted. I believe that the prayer she prayed for me, she prayed daily for herself. We couldn't help who we are, her being a widow and myself being a homosexual, and we both faced the same debilitating judgement of the church.

At the time, there was a man in the congregation who had the voice of an angel; he would sing beautifully on the altar of the church. The entire congregation knew he was gay; it wasn't long before he was asked to step down from worship leader. At times, though, they still needed him to fill in, and the days when he sang, it was as though God entered the building in all his glory. They used him because of his talent, but when push came to shove, he was treated as an outsider as well. For instance, he was never allowed to sing if an important preacher was coming to town.

It wasn't long before the church had people approach us, individually and together, to tell us that we should get together and form a relationship. The church had previously tried to set him up with women who were considered trouble so that they could demonstrate that he wasn't gay in order to utilise his talent further. It's crazy; the church thought that if they could just get us to be together, our homosexuality would go away.

He was such a lovely guy; I could see how the church was hurting him, as they were hurting me. Each time they suggested something of this nature, it made him feel inadequate, like he was never enough to satisfy the church, which wanted him to compromise himself. It was incidents such as these that made me question the integrity of this holy sanctuary and the meaning of a sanctuary in the first place. What was the point in coming here to meet with God only to deal with the judgements of people and the ludicrous demands they would set in the name of God? There is no love in acts such as these, and I have learnt that the hard way. What is presented in the disguise of love and concern is actually a security measure to maintain a distorted and judgemental belief.

My question to the church is, how could it ever be wrong in the eyes of God to love and accept us as we are?

There were many days I looked up with tears rolling down my

face and said, "Enough is enough." One day, I couldn't do it anymore. I couldn't deal with the church's demands that I change myself. Making two homosexuals of the opposite sex get together could never change their sexuality or their sexual preference. In fact, it causes them to live a lie and hurt a lot more people along the way. Of all the solutions for gay reparative therapy, this has to be the most ridiculous.

Writing this story brought back so much anger I had for the church at the time. I was so incredibly angry for the lack of respect, lack of consideration, and most importantly, lack of love. When I listen to the voice of God in regards to the church, I'm guided towards compassion, with the understanding that all negativity stems from ignorance. Forgive them, Father, for they know not what they do. May your love penetrate ignorance and expand the hearts of those who seek to exclude any of your children.

CHAPTER 6

Inside Gay Rehab

I WAS READY for a solution to this "problem" of sexual preference. I decided to confide in a long-time family friend, who happened to be attending the same Pentecostal church as me. I braced her for a big confession as we sat down over coffee. After telling her that I was gay and currently dating a woman, she was unable to speak for a time. She told me that she didn't judge me and that all sins were the same to her, and yet she also told me within the same breath that I could not continue down this path if I wanted to live for God. I was sad and told her that I loved my partner and didn't want to leave her, but that I loved God too. She agreed with the youth leader that I should take on the programs available to me through the church to get rid of these desires. She also said she would be a support during the process.

Having pondered everything that was going on, I decided I would fight this "demon," as they often called it, with all my might. I was going to beat this, if not for me, for the suffering I might bring my family. The first treatment was a weekend at a retreat in the mountains, where people went for serious healings. I met some interesting people: people dying of cancer, victims of debilitating accidents, and people going through abusive marriages. I was treated like a leper there, as my issue was considered the worst of them all and, apparently, the hardest one to heal. The sessions consisted of singing hymns, praying, private counselling sessions, exorcisms (for me, anyway), and group sharing.

The first private session was with a male and female pastor; they wanted to know about my upbringing and my relationships. I found it really hard and remember feeling so ashamed because they questioned me on sorts of private and personal matters, such as if I masturbated and how frequently, if I watched porn, how often I thought about women in a sexual way, how long it had been since I was in a relationship, what the relationship was like, and whether we had sex regularly. The questions were so personal. I felt shame with every response, but I was doing this to be healed, and they were encouraging my absolute honesty, telling me that without it, they couldn't fulfil their duties.

Once they had finished the interrogation, I was told that Jesus died to wash away all my sins and that he would cleanse me of all I had participated in, if I never did it again and either chose a life of celibacy or married a man. They also regularly told me that I wasn't a lesbian and that I should repeat this in my mind as often as possible.

I was so glad when the session was over; I couldn't believe how open and honest I had been, yet I didn't feel any better for it. We had a break before lunch; I went to a nearby field and looked at the blue sky, silently observing the beautiful countryside and wildlife. I thought about what I was doing and wept. Was this really possible? It felt like my heart had been pierced right through, but I assumed it was due to the work being done. Maybe it was a miracle, and my heart was finally changing. We were called into lunch and sat around each other, completely bewildered. None of us really spoke to one another; if their sessions were anything like mine, I could understand why no one wanted to talk.

The woman sitting next to me smiled and asked, "Could you pass the salt?"

"Sure," I responded.

"What are you here for?" she asked.

I signalled for her to come closer so no one else could hear. "I'm gay," I told her.

She looked a little shocked, and I rolled my eyes, feeling as though I was about to receive more criticism, but instead, she asked, "But weren't you born that way?"

It was the first time someone had asked me that, and I responded that I wasn't sure. I really wasn't. She said, "I could be wrong, but I don't think homosexuality is healable."

I was saddened by the fact that she thought it may not be healable, but she also made me think about the concept of being born this way. I was finally able to ask myself whether it was meant to be. What if?

After lunch, there was a group sharing session; of course, my issue was by far the worst, and I realised that. I was not allowed to participate in the group discussion. I listened to all their stories and saw how much pain these people were in and how desperately they were seeking a miracle for their sickness or predicament. I had nothing but compassion for them and wished for their healing miracle to come true for them. There was a man who had been in a bad accident, and his arm had been mutilated. He was there with his wife as support; they were praying and hoping that God could give him an entire new arm or give him the courage and strength to live with the one he now had. The man was suffering with a deep depression because he felt he couldn't live, feeling the way he did.

It was time for session number two, and this one was about my upbringing, in the hope that they could find the root cause of why homosexuality had "happened" to me. I told them about my sexual abuse as a child, and they immediately made the decision that this was why I was the way I was. I told them that I don't hate men, and they kept saying it's understandable that I would hate men. I kept reiterating that I don't hate men; in fact, I have so many beautiful men in my life, men I love deeply, including my father. They were adamant that this caused it all. The man who had molested me somehow invoked my own sexual perversion, being lesbian. I was happy in a way, as it felt like they found a solution. If they found the cause, surely they had the solution planned. I was wrong. They didn't know what to do and simply stated that I was molested, and the outcome was lesbianism.

I suggested that if this man was the reason I am a lesbian, and he had somehow made me "perverse," then surely this perverse spirit could be exorcised. They thought that this was a great idea, and so they prayed and asked for the perverted demon to exit my body. They used prayers like "In Jesus' name, I command you to leave this woman."

I don't know what I expected. I thought something would override me, talk to them in a freakish voice, maybe even turn my head 360 degrees before waking up healed. Nothing strange happened (for me, anyway). All the weird voices and "speaking in tongues" was all coming from them. I was just sitting there, waiting for it to be over. It was dinner time now; these sessions took hours. Everyone looked far more exhausted than they had looked at lunch. Trying to have a normal conversation was hard, and considering the circumstances, we really didn't know what to say to one another.

I didn't sleep that night. I spent most of it talking to God: "Why on earth did I come here? What was I hoping to achieve?" Nothing felt different. I still felt like me. I watched the sunrise, and it was beautiful; the scenery was gorgeous, and I felt God's peaceful and comforting presence in those early hours, looking at the mountains and watching the animals.

The next day, I was more talkative, and we all discussed the Bible. They were a little shocked that a lesbian knew so much about God's word. They were impressed at my knowledge and asked if I had studied. I told them that I had studied the Bible for some time but not through a university or anything. I had done a couple of courses, but nothing major. I received my knowledge from reading the Bible, the books removed from the Bible, history in relation to the Bible, and any books I could find surrounding the Bible; in particular, I really studied sexuality in the Bible.

The next day involved sharing stories and talking about how much better we feel and how God has begun to work in us. I didn't feel any different, just as the man who had lost his limb didn't have a new arm.

I was discouraged but still hopeful because I still had ex-gay ministry to do. This had to work; they specialised in homosexuality, after all. This course was conducted over a period of fifty-two weeks, one to two days per week, at a secret location. I asked why the location was secret (it was only given to us a few hours before), and the response was that gay communities fought against such reparative therapies.

On the first day, after completing our introductions (the group consisted of mostly men and three women, including myself), we had to fill out some very personal forms. It was a checklist of why you might be gay. The checklist consisted of questions like, Were you molested? By who, male or female? At what age were you molested? Were you an only child? Did your father and mother want the opposite sex when you were born? What Christian background did you come from? What gender do you feel like inside? And so on.

I answered the questions. Once we had finished the formalities, the male leader of the group asked how everyone felt about the form and the questions they just answered, suggesting that this form was a list of the probable "whys" of our sexuality.

I put my hand up and said, "I only have one issue with this form."

He seemed shocked and a little embarrassed; he asked, "Oh, well, what is it?"

"I have a friend who has experienced almost everything I have, to the letter, and we even come from the same background," I replied. "In some respects, her situation was far worse than mine, and she is perfectly straight."

There was silence in the room; he dodged the question by saying that it was a great topic, but it was time to get into our groups. Men and women separated for the sessions, then we came back together for coffee and some hymns at the end. This course was no joke; it presented an in-depth review on how and why homosexuality is possible, listing the following reasons:

1. Studies on how humans can only be born straight, and that showing traits of the opposite gender means nothing and can be corrected early on.
2. Studies on how a baby receives identity from its father and comfort from the mother. If something at birth has gone awry, then this could be a cause.
3. Studies on how single parenting can be the cause.
4. Studies on how a healthy sexuality, when interfered with by trauma such as molestation, bullying, or an accident, could be the cause.
5. Our neuro-linguistic programming could be the cause: how our brain is wired.
6. Studies on how family circumstances could be the cause, such as abandonment.
7. Studies on how a rebellious nature stems from Adam and Eve.
8. Studies on what the Bible says about homosexuality.
9. Scriptures that will help in the "deliverance and healing" of homosexuality.
10. Asking God for miracles.

The course was intense; these were just some of the subjects. The program was headed by a preacher who "used to be" gay and was on his way to becoming a woman. He had started his own church, married a woman, and lived a heterosexual life. It's interesting because if you met him or heard him speak, you wouldn't believe he is straight. He says he is now a man, a feminine man, but a man nonetheless. I actually don't care about his sexuality or what it is he claims to be. I do, however, feel terribly sorry for the people who have gone through his program. I wonder if he knows how many kids have committed suicide because of their failure to change. Again, that's not for me to judge. In the words of Gandhi, I believe humans are all so uniquely messed up, how could we possible judge one another?

In this group, the male leader had chosen to get married and have children, and he claimed to be free from homosexuality. During confession, which was part of the sessions (usually at the end), he confessed to caving in to watching gay porn. I wondered why he thought he was healed.

In one session, a question was asked about relationships and who had acted out on their homosexual feelings. I found it interesting that only the three married men in the group put up their hands. I decided to be honest and told the group that I had acted out on my feelings, had been in relationships with women, and had sex with them.

The group was silent, and the leaders left with mouths open. I didn't care. I felt as though this was my last option, and I wasn't going to lie about anything because I needed real answers. My reply encouraged another member of the group to put up his hand and admit he had acted out and slept with a man. That was as far as it went: Four honest people in a group of twenty.

The female leader in the group had chosen to remain single and live a life of celibacy, which I personally do not consider an option. I enjoy people too much and wanted love in my life. I wanted sex as well, to be frank. In all honesty, this leader wasn't a picture of happiness herself and seemed like she could use a good orgasm or two. She had a great voice; I would watch her sing, and as she was singing hymns to God, tears would roll down her face, as though she was trying to give her suffering to God. I admired her strength, but it seemed to me that God couldn't remove the pain she had chosen for herself. Each tear that fell represented every guilty, shameful, distorted idea about herself.

I had reached the end of my rope. I was done trying to change. I was done fighting it and decided to just let it be. Come what may,

I could not go through any more therapy. I tried healing with the church, healing retreats, and now ex gay ministry. I spent almost five years of my life being single so I wouldn't drag anyone through my healing process (and, of course, because it would defeat the purpose). After five years of trying to fix something that clearly could not be repaired, it seemed to me the purpose was already defeated. I was doomed, and that was it. I had tried everything I possibly could, and nothing worked. I had no hope and was at the depths of my despair. I couldn't do it anymore. I wanted to lie down and just die; after all, without love, what do we have to live for?

I remember watching a documentary on Matthew Shepard, who was murdered because he was gay. His death changed the nation (and even the world). He was an attractive, everyday young American in his freshman year at college; this image made Americans think this could have been their son. As I watched this documentary in absolute horror of what had occurred, what was more horrifying was the reaction from the church. Christian protesters were at his funeral, holding signs that said "Fags go to hell" and "God hates fags." I was mortified.

A few weeks prior to the brutal beating that led to his death, Matthew had attended a local church near his campus, seeking help and answers. In response, a woman told him he was going to hell and that he was a disgrace in the eyes of God. I cried for days after watching this documentary because I too had sought refuge in the church, only to be told that God did not love me.

I feel it necessary in this chapter to stress the point that God loves all of us, gay or straight, black or white, priest or murderer. We are *all* creations of God. Back in the 1990s, church people told me that homosexuals were only 5 percent of this planet, and so we must be a bad seed: an error made by God or made by our parents and their sins. Back then, when the world's population was six billion people, I calculated that 5 percent would equal three hundred million people. How could God make an error with that many people?

In this documentary, Matthew's church handled his situation like mine did: with such a lack of love. This always confused me because the God I know is all about love and inclusion. Matthew's parents decided that in order to bring healing to their situation, they would not seek the death penalty for the murderers. These convicted murderers would have to thank them (or Matthew) for their lives.

I learnt such a valuable lesson from their story, and that is to always show compassion, especially to the people who need it the most. I have said it before that it is not my goal to shame the church; my or motivation is to bring light to a dark place within the church, in the hope that we can all learn to love each other better.

CHAPTER 7

Coming Out

"WE MUST LET go of what we *think* we are to get to who we really are." – Lenita Vangellis

I am always and forever confused with this subject of coming out. Life is a journey, and we are forever discovering ourselves. There is this idea in society, and even in the gay community, that a moment should arrive when you admit to the world who you really are, specifically your sexuality, and this moment of coming out is only necessary if you do not identify with being heterosexual. I don't believe that such a moment is necessary.

This thought would always cross my mind: Do straight people come out to say that they are straight? Do artists come out and say that they are artists? The list could go on and on here. Where did this need to limit via category come from? I have mentioned already that I don't find anything of value in labels. Labels only limit and separate, and I am a firm believer in unity. We are one. Whether you're black, white, Asian, gay, straight, tall, short, skinny, or curvy, you still bleed red. One of society's greatest barriers to understanding homosexuality is the inability to accept each other as unique individuals, without placing judgement on the very nature that makes us unique.

A very good friend of mine is a light-skinned black, and I remember being out with her for coffee when a lady came up to me and whispered in my ear, "You know she is black, right?"

I nearly spat my coffee out. I couldn't believe my ears. I told Jane shortly after what the woman had said and then went quiet, not knowing what to say. Jane explained to me that she deals with this all the time. I was so shocked. I gave her an enormous hug and kiss, a bigger one than usual, and said that we live in a world full of shitty people. I didn't know what else to say (that was probably not the right thing).

This incident brought me back to my childhood in primary school. Mum had moved us to a very Aussie neighbourhood because she didn't want us to only mingle with Italians, like many of the communities where we lived. I believe now more than ever that Mum made an insightfully good decision. It all starts with one person: yourself. You alone can make a difference that travels down generations. At school, we were teased for being immigrants and called wogs, and this caused the blacks, the Indians, the Asians, and anyone else who looked different to become our friends.

This may sound really strange, but over the years, it was food that brought the Aussies into my world. Mum would invite the parents of other students over for coffee or cake; she was rejected many times, but eventually, they came around and realised that we are all just the same. This life lesson taught me a great deal about the judgements we create about people and ourselves. I never wanted anyone else to feel what I felt, being rejected because of my ethnicity, and so I made sure to make everyone feel loved and accepted, no matter who they were or what their background was.

In year three at primary school, I had a run-in with a group of girls. I am quite the clown, and I just love people. As a kid, I expressed this trait more noticeably. A group of girls pinned me up against a wall and were teasing me for being a wog. One of the girls, the leader of the mean girls group, had me by the throat. I couldn't breathe and panicked; I didn't know what to do (those who know me know I wouldn't hurt a fly), but in my struggle, I kicked the girl in the stomach. I kicked her hard enough that she let go.

This incident was pretty huge; our parents were called in, and the principal told my mother that I had kicked another girl in the stomach. My mother knew my gentle nature and said that something must have happened for me to react this way. I had tears in my eyes, thinking I was in trouble, as Mum asked me what happened.

I told the principal that the girl had me by the neck and I couldn't breathe; as I grabbed my neck in re-enactment, I realised it was sore. Mum noticed I had red marks, like those similar to a rope burn, from one side of my neck to the other.

Well, I had never seen my mum react in such a way. My neck had blood vessels come to the surface, and I just remember my mother blasting the principal so badly that it was actually the leader of the mean girls who would now be in trouble. This next part of the incident says a lot about upbringing and how our prejudices are not our own; in a way, we are trained to believe and think a certain way. The principal asked for the other girl and her parents to enter the office and explained why I had kicked their daughter. In shock, they disciplined her in front of me and told her never to do it again.

My mum looked at the young girl with compassion and asked, "Little girl, do you even know what 'wog' means?"

She responded that she didn't; it was something she had heard her parents say. Her father was a friend of my father; I couldn't believe that he had such resentment towards "wogs" and yet could be friends with my dad. It was a lesson for everyone that day; her parents apologised to my mum. When Mum told Dad about what had taken place, he could not believe that his friend felt this way about wogs. He chose to remain friends with the man and hoped that he would come around in his ways. Dad showed him compassion.

Several years later, we were in high school, and this very same girl came up to me one day and asked if I recalled the incident from when we were children. I said that I did. She expressed how sorry she was and said that she always wondered where that hatred came from. She felt the need to tell me how sorry she was. I was silent for a few seconds because it was so long ago, and I couldn't believe that it was still weighing on her. I told her that we had been children, and children do stupid things. I also told her that I forgave her and thanked her for apologising.

There is so much power in forgiveness. This girl taught me to never be afraid to admit fault and apologise. It takes courage to do that, and I admired her for it. More importantly, I admired that she had grown up and realised that there was hatred inside her and had let it go.

There was a time at church when I was asked to go back into the closet until I sorted myself out. I'll never forget this. It made me question a lot about myself and the God I believed in. "Going back in the closet" for church was really their way of saying we don't accept you as you are, and if you want to be here, don't show people who you really are. A pastor I admired spent some time with me; in fact, many people from church throughout the years took it upon themselves to "save" me. I could never work out what they meant when they said I was now saved.

I believe Jesus wanted us to live like him so that we could save ourselves. Jesus' example is salvation in itself. Christians often spend so much time worrying about the rituals and interpretations of Christianity that they forget to actually be like Christ.

With the many church therapies I took part in, the hardest thing for me to accept was the church's belief that I had a serious perversion. In the eyes of the church, homosexuals are viewed on the same level as rapists, paedophiles, and sex addicts. This hurt me, but ironically, it was my saving grace, as I was able to see the error of this perspective. It didn't sit right in my heart. A lot of the therapy didn't sit right within my heart, and I knew that the church had this wrong. They had to have it wrong. In *The Little Prince*, the writer often refers to seeing things through your heart. This was a time in my life where I had to do this, and it was life or death. I had to try to look at myself through my own heart and evaluate who I really was in order to decide what I believed about myself.

The subject of perversion really got me thinking. This is not meant to be funny, but there was a black comedy to this story. I had made friends with a lot of women and men at church, and they would open up to me and tell me their deepest, darkest secrets. I wondered why this was happening and actually asked a couple of them, and their answers were astonishing to me. They thought that because my sin was considered one of the worst, they could share their sins, which were not "as bad" as mine.

These stories were seriously shocking, and without going into detail, they often involved unusual or uncommon forms of sex, adultery, sexual fantasies that involved animals, drug abuse, drug dealing, stealing, and fraud. There were many times when I would say to myself, *It's you who needs therapy, not me.*

There was a period when I was in a relationship and deeply in love, and I would constantly compare the examples I was given to my own life. It also got me thinking a lot about love. What is love in its purest form? If we look at Jesus' example, it is clear that he really loved everyone. He gave to everyone, he didn't fear anyone (not even those who killed him), and he didn't judge anyone. His love had even transcended sexuality, which must have seemed to him a strange and superficial expression of love. He didn't need special and exclusive relationships to teach him about love, for he was love. Sexuality was likely redundant for him, replaced with a loving intimacy for all living things.

Maybe one day, we will all move past exclusive relationships and sexuality, but for now, it seems we still have a lot more to learn from them. I've learnt a lot about love over the years, and I know I will keep learning until the day I die. I feel like we are all here to learn about love, how to experience it, how to cherish it, and how to share it. I feel like it is actually our only true lesson in life. We all wonder what our purpose is in life, but if that purpose doesn't stem from love, then is it really worth it? Most inspirational people simply followed love. All inspirational figures have one thing in common: The world was moved by their love, in one form or another.

We still have much to learn from romantic love. I believe making love is sacred and involves the sharing of energy in such a profound way that when we are awake and aware, it becomes increasingly difficult to be sexual with someone without love. Sex is an act of love, and it exists so that our love may evolve, maybe even beyond sex.

One of the beliefs I dealt with (and sometimes still struggle with today) is that I shouldn't have sex with women because it wouldn't be "right," and yet I have had beautiful sexual experiences with women whom I have loved deeply. In the spiritual experience of sex, two souls merge and become one. For all the Christians who believe this is not possible for same-sex couples, I have news for you (ancient news, but news nonetheless): This experience is what makes sex meaningful and is in no way restricted to heterosexual intimacy. It's so bizarre, but in one of my therapy sessions, it was claimed that souls merge during sex but only the bad traits rubbed off on one another, not the good, and it was an unlawful merger. When you love someone, even on a friendship level, you can't help but share aspects of each other. This is human connection, and it intensifies on a romantic level. What is shared between the two depends on their individual feelings and intents in expressing them. Intimacy can also be shared between friends, same sex or otherwise. I feel it necessary to share an experience of my own in regards to romantic love.

I attended a conference, and as I walked from my car into the conference room, my heart was beating heavily. I could feel it through my shirt. It was an unusual experience, and I thought it was odd that I stopped to notice my own heartbeat. It was almost as though my heart knew who was coming into my life, and this was its way of telling me she was special. I had met several people at the entrance to the conference, but when I shook hands with this one woman, we looked into each other's eyes, and there was silence. The handshake seemed slow motion, and we both struggled to say hello. She welcomed me to the conference, and I thanked her while trying to get my hand back, but she was holding onto it pretty tight.

She released my hand, and I smiled as I went to my seat. As I walked to my seat, I looked back at her a couple times, and we both caught each other staring. I sat down in my seat, wondering what just happened, and the event began. I could see where she was sitting, and I could see her trying to look around the room to, I suppose, find me. She eventually did, and we both smiled.

I was sitting by myself, and about halfway through the event, she made her way over to me and asked if she could sit next to me. I agreed, and we began talking. She was fascinating and seemed really interested, asking me lots of questions about myself. It was a Christian conference, and we discussed what we were doing there and had many discussions about God.

I wonder if she knows we are flirting, I thought. It wouldn't be the first time that a woman was attracted by my sexuality, drawing me in for the fun of it, only to tell me that she is straight. Yes, I have had this quite a bit. I have had many woman play with the idea, only to tell me no or that they want it just for the experience, as though I'm some sort of crash test dummy.

I knew, however, this was different. There was something there. When she spoke, electricity flowed from her to me; there was chemistry. My heart told me to take it slow, and so we met up for coffee and spoke a lot on the phone. I would get these feelings and call her, and she would say it was weird because she was just thinking of me. A lot of synchronicities happen when things are meant to be.

As time went on, she became more affectionate and spoke to me differently. She would tell me that she missed me, and her body language said she wanted more out of our friendship. I decided I wouldn't make the first move. It was hard for me at times because I knew in my heart, it was what she wanted, but I knew I had to wait until she was ready. The first person I came out to was myself, and I could see that she was having this moment in her life, and so I waited.

A friend of mine at the time had asked me how I could feel so strongly even though nothing physical had happened between us. I believe that our spirit knows who it wants, and it is our body and mind that need to catch up. Just like in *The Alchemist*, I knew I loved her before I got to know her. Simply knowing her expanded my love.

One night, she knocked at my door: an unexpected visit. As I opened the door to ask if everything was okay, she kissed me. That night, we didn't have sex, but we felt incredible intimacy while kissing for what felt like the entire evening until early morning. We were one with each other and one with everything else. I know this may be hard for some people to believe, but it was far better than an orgasm. Love can take you places the mind can only dream of. I will always remember that kiss as one of the most beautiful moments I have ever experienced. Another moment, we both had tears at the same time, overwhelmed by the love that we were feeling. I knew at this moment what the alchemist meant when he said that he loved her because the universe "conspired" to bring them together.

Like most beautiful things in life, humans always find a way to cheapen them. Pornography, for example, removes the emotion and becomes something we do to one another, as opposed to something we share with one another. Love in its purest form is beautiful, and I don't know that I have experienced the best of it, but this time was pretty close. Even though we are no longer together, I will always love her, and I pray that she may see herself as God sees her. This is my prayer for all who are struggling with beliefs surrounding their sexuality, and my prayer for us all. May we let go of all the little ideas, stifling limitations, and destructive illusions about ourselves. May we see each other and ourselves for the light we are. May we see what God sees.

After a while, she felt she needed to make a decision in her heart.

She had to choose between a relationship with me or one with God. She chose God, and I am happy for her, if that brought her happiness. If not, may she have the courage to believe she can choose again and choose differently.

CHAPTER 8

Gay Community

WHILE I WAS coming out, I never quite fit in to the gay community. There weren't as many "lipsticks" as there are now, and I wanted to keep my femininity, as it was important to me. I never wanted to cut my hair short, get tattoos, and buy a Harley; that is not who I am. I loved being a woman. I loved my long hair, my curves, and my fake nails. I couldn't conform in this way and found it hard to be part of the gay community because of this. I felt like I didn't fit into those stereotypes, which seemed unavoidable. It bothers me a little that we even need a community because of our sexuality, although I acknowledge that such communities have helped homosexuals on their journey. I stress here that I understand the need for the community, and as long as humanity requires us to be separate from the rest, we may still need it, for extra support. My hope is that one day, all of this will dissipate, and we will live in a world where there is only one prevalent belief system: that we are all one, we are all unique, we are all loved and accepted by society, and we are all free to be ourselves.

I understand the need for contrasts on this earth plane. Without them, life would be boring, and we would have nothing to compare ourselves to. A good friend of mine once said that our core essence is divine; this is true, but we also believe that we are human, and whilst we live on this earth plane in these physical bodies, we must face the constant push and pull of duality, the seemingly endless lessons of growth to move past our self-imposed limitations. I've learnt a lot from Jesus; he has been an inspiration for me in my life. Jesus is a great example of what it looks like to accept, love, and bless people of all walks of life, irrespective of their culture, their beliefs, their sexuality, or their status.

The most beautiful people and true representations of Christ I have met generally have not been participants at church; instead, they have been people who express themselves freely and progressively, are at peace with themselves, and choose to embody peace and love without dogma. Religious dogma is so dangerous because religion is meant to set us free, not limit us with superfluous, irrelevant, and distorted interpretations of a very simple message: love. Christ never spoke about homosexuality. My personal belief is that he isn't interested in romantic love. He is interested in universal love.

In 2012, I became great friends with some women who worked at the local Thai massage place in town. I'm not sure how the connection happened, but we began speaking about spirituality, and they shared their beliefs. One of the girls grew up in a Christian convent run by a group of nuns, although her original religion was Buddhism. She expressed how greatly blessed she was to learn about two great spiritual teachers and relayed her understandings on how they both connect. It wasn't long before we became such close friends that they would come over for family dinners; my entire family enjoyed the conversations. I learnt so much from them in terms of spirituality. They were both on a search for deeper meaning and understanding of this strange and wonderful journey called life.

I had many profound experiences with them; one in particular changed everything for me. I had never had someone explain mindfulness to me quite like her. She would take me on a meditation like journey and ask me when I last listened to my heart, when I last took the time to feel the grass or even the road under my feet, when I last felt the breeze and listened to it, when I last examined the skin I'm in and noticed its texture and sensation.

She explained that prayer is being present and knowing yourself. It is only through awareness of the present moment that we can separate from the left hemisphere of our brain, which is constantly analysing, categorising, and projecting into the past and future. With practice, the clashing voices of ego and spirit start to become distinct and separate, as we learn to identify with spirit instead of the ego. She further described that prayer is about knowing and not about asking. I had always known prayer to be a list of things I needed God to help me with, or problems that needed sorting out. I never thought about prayer in this way. I now see how important the ancient proverb of "Know thyself" is, for to know our true self is disassociation with the ego and identity in love, remembering that we are divine and have never lost our connection to God.

I have several trans friends and feel it vital to mention my friend's story in this chapter, as she (who was born a he) never felt like she fit in to the gay community, either. I interviewed her for this book, to review my opinions on trans to see if it felt right to her; I gained a deeper understanding of how important it is for us to see each other as souls. One of the first questions I asked her was when and how she started with treatment. She was the first trans I ever met who decided not to take on hormone treatment; her explanation for this was, "I know who I am. I don't need medication to affirm that for me. I always knew I was a woman; my physicality is what it is. I cannot help that and do not want to change that. I am a female born with male anatomy, but nevertheless, I am female."

I was blown away; after knowing her for some time, I actually could not see the male aspect. She is a woman, and a woman is all I saw; a woman is all the energy expressed from her. I love that she has decided to "be herself" without medication, but this was a highly personal choice that may not be relevant for others on a similar journey. We discussed many subjects, and one of her stories really stood out for me. It explains a lot about our upbringing and the imprinting (or programming) instilled by those around us.

She told me a story about her childhood; she played with other little girls and naturally fit in with them. She always referred to herself as a girl from as far back as she can remember. What made her understand at that age that she was different was when gifts were being distributed; she would always get a blue-coloured item or a male toy, and not the pink items or a girl toy. What an interesting example of how we are conditioned a certain way. I mean, what if a little girl's favourite colour was actually blue. It's such a small example of conditioning, but for my friend, it made her understand that even though she perceived herself as a girl, no one around her saw her that way.

It has only been in recent years that she decided she wanted to be herself and dress accordingly. Of all the changes she tried, including using drag to feel female, she found her peace and acceptance through being the woman she always knew she was. She entered my apartment for my interview with her wearing skinny jeans, funky boots with heels, a stylish sweater, and a blazer, with her hair straightened and a full face of makeup. I realised that she was just like my other female friends. She moved, spoke, and looked like them, and her gentle, nurturing demeanour made me feel like she was just like me: a woman.

Many parts of her story were sad; one in particular was when she described relationships. In the midst of a heavy conversation, we had a laugh about Usher lyrics, wanting "a lady in the street but a freak in the bed." In her situation, it was the complete opposite. The straight men she dated wanted a lady in the bedroom, but outside the bedroom, they considered her a freak. I mentioned that the men she dated were straight (some would argue this point). This brings me back to my comment that sexuality is deeper and more complex than we can imagine; sooner or later, we will discover that it can only be deciphered through spirit. If she considers herself a woman and wants to be with a man, then it would only make sense that she would want a straight man: a man who desired women. There are many men out there who can look beyond the physicality and accept the woman in front of them. This subject is difficult for many to understand but freedom doesn't come from holding onto our fears. It is the fear of all that is rare and uniquely different that causes judgement, which inevitably leads to separation.

People don't often think about these issues until it happens within their own families, and in my own experience, the people who have been hard on me the most had issues within themselves or their own families. There was one woman in particular who was so hard on me and so determined to get me healed that she performed rituals and held prayer meetings for me, and all of those actions stemmed from the fact that her own sister was a lesbian, and she felt that if she could heal me, she could heal her sister. There was one time in church I heard the preacher use the word "faggot" straight off the pulpit. His message was delivered with such aggression; later on, it was discovered his own son was gay, and he wasn't coping with that.

I'd like to add a story here about a priest in the uniting church whose daughter is gay; instead of listening to the congregation and the judgements of others, he decided to embrace her and love her for who she is. This priest was controversial for a while, but once people got over it, he actually became a pillar of hope for the gay community. Because of him, many young and old homosexuals who had been forced to leave the church went back, regained their faith, and began a new relationship with God and themselves.

I was privileged to meet this man; he was such an inspiration to me. There were times he appeared uncomfortable, but he persevered because of the love he had for his daughter. What a great example of the power of love. Through the actions of this man, people saw a true aspect of God, one who loves unconditionally, even if at times he struggled with the technicalities. Sometimes love, real love, means stepping out into the unknown and going with what spirit is telling you, regardless of the fear you might feel. A congregation of traditionalists may have walked out but an entire group of kids and adults hungry for God walked in.

I don't know about all the pastors and priests out there, but wouldn't you want a church that was truly hungry for God? This story showed me how important faith is, as well as our belief in something greater than our individual selves. Faith is so important that when members have been rejected from church for their sexuality, it has often led to suicide; that tells you just how important believing in something is and the need to share that sense of purpose and belonging with others. Sometimes, you don't know how important something is until it's taken away from you. In all my experiences, the more I was rejected, the more God would penetrate my heart and show me what real love is. I'm extremely blessed and so grateful for his love and that my negative experiences in church did not rattle my faith. To know God is to know divine love, for that is what he is.

I want to express my gratitude to the LGBT community for how much they have contributed to our acceptance and the moving forward of prejudices in society. In saying that, I hope and pray that we do not become like other institutions, as I fear that at times, we have been guilty of such. Our mottos include "Love is love," "Equality," and "Acceptance." Let us not forget that it is for ALL humanity that these slogans must be expressed. We cannot be about segregation, for we will make the same mistakes as every other institution. It is my prayer that through what we have all been through, we can receive the words "Love is love" to heart and truly believe in their meaning. When there is segregation and exclusion, we are no longer a community; we are no longer united, and we are no longer about love, for love *is* unity. Sexuality is broad, diverse, complex, and universally shared; this is why it should not be confined to specific groups, labels, or categories. It should be intuitive, trusting, and free flowing, like life itself.

My entire life I wanted to be a fashion designer and artist and I know it sounds crazy (a wannabe fashion designer and artist throwing labels out the window), but as we evolve as humans, the labels that separate us will eventually disappear. I hope this beautiful world of peace, love, and acceptance is made manifest in my lifetime.

Based on the fact that not every woman feels she belongs or fits into the gay community, I feel it necessary to share a story here. After people knew about my sexuality and my stand in terms of being myself and not changing to conform to how people think a lesbian should look or behave, I began to attract women who were older. Most of them were married. I met one woman who was in her fifties who politely asked me out and told me she just wanted a sexual relationship. She wanted to be with a woman sexually because most men were not able to satisfy her or give her what she wanted. I was single at the time and so agreed to a strictly physical relationship. Women know women's bodies, and so we have an advantage in this respect. We know what we like; we know the signs of pleasure and how to read each other.

I felt for her, as she had confided in me that her ex-husband hadn't managed to help her reach orgasm and so forth. Our relationship turned out, as always, to be founded on a lot more than just the physical; we spent the majority of our time together engaged in deep conversation. I realised, though, that this woman really only wanted an orgasm; she didn't actually want me. She had begun explaining how she loved women and believed she may be a lesbian, but I had to stop her. I said that although I could not answer the question of who she was, I knew she was not a lesbian.

I asked her if she ever expressed herself to her ex-husband, in particular how she felt, how she craved sex, and how she wanted sex to be performed. To my amazement, she never had such discussions with him. I thought it sad to be in a marriage and not really know each other. I gave her some advice that with her next boyfriend she should try and talk to him and express what she wants and how she wants it.

She soon found herself dating a man, and now they are happy, and she is satisfied sexually. I knew she wasn't gay; to this day, she thanks me for not pushing the sexuality question on her and helping her find who she really was. I knew that although she sought love and satisfaction, she didn't want me; she just felt comfortable talking to me.

Women are great conversationalists and nurturers, and so I suppose she felt comfortable enough to share her fantasies and enjoy a sexual experience. We still keep in touch, and she tells me from time to time that it was so simple and yet so complicated; if she had just had the courage to speak to her husband at the time, they could have had the perfect marriage. Of course, this is not always the case; this is just one example. I have met married women who have admitted the truth to themselves after years of marriage and felt trapped, not knowing how to handle the situation. They blamed themselves, with the reasoning that if only they had been true to themselves earlier on, they would have saved a lot of people pain, namely their husbands. This is a sad truth in some ways, but seemingly difficult situations always urge us onwards in the search for our truest self.

Another story I would like to talk about here was one of my biggest challenges in terms of accepting others. It was also my biggest personal hurdle. When I was a child and experienced a near-death experience, it was as though God had downloaded information into me. I knew things beyond my years. I understood energy in a way others didn't; people often looked at me strangely.

Near where I grew up was a family who were devout born-again Christians. They really shaped my life in many ways, and today, I am grateful for them, but I didn't always feel this way. I connected with the mother of the family, who made the big move from her Religion to Christianity. She was shunned by her community and pretty much excommunicated by them and by her devout family. She knew a bit about God, and that was the beginning of our connection.

She could see I was hungry for God, and although she admired that in me, she would also be jealous at times. There were times I would ask her a question in Bible study, and she would get so angry with me because she didn't know how to answer my very deep and profound question. I was constantly teeming with questions. "Why did Jesus do this?" and "What does that mean?" kind of questions, and it infuriated her because people in organised religions often want you to just believe without "knowing." I could never be satisfied with this blind faith and wanted my relationship with God to be experiential and real.

To be honest, after my NDE, I craved the love of God so deeply but couldn't find it in any church or sect of Christianity I tried, and I tried a lot. Something was missing from them all. During my NDE, I had seen a realm where we are all one and united under the banner of love, and I came back to a reality that didn't accept my idea of love, as it didn't fit within the rigid framework of organised religion. I would often look at this woman's life and wonder why God would ever want to separate her from her family and the community she grew up in. Her own siblings were shunned because they didn't convert to Christianity, which in her eyes was the one true religion. I believe that one day, when we all wake up, we will discover that the one true religion is love. Love is who God is, and love is who we are in truth, and that is the only reality I ever want to accept in my life. Organised religion is bondage.

I will never forget my experiences with her. She was the person who convinced me that I was sick and needed healing from my homosexuality. I once thought that she was my greatest curse, when actually, she was a blessing, and I thank her for the gift which led me to find my true self.

I remember my mother would always tell me to be careful of this lady, and I would ask Mum why. Mum told me that this woman once kicked her out of Bible study because she couldn't speak in tongues. For those who don't know what speaking in tongues means, it's when the Holy Spirit grants people permission to speak and understand the language of heaven. I cannot speak in tongues, although I have had many dreams where I experienced meditations and received words I did not understand. Christians have a habit of making people feel less than if they have not received these gifts.

I remember once in a meditation, I asked God, "Why can't I have this gift so I can fit in at church, and why couldn't you give the gift to my mother so that she didn't get kicked out of Bible study?"

The response I received astounded me: "The only language we need to know both here on earth and here in Spirit is the language of love. This love does not require interpretation, and although it is a gift, it does not need to be earned, for it has been yours always. There is nothing you must do to receive a gift from God. God is a gift to you, and you are a gift to God; there is no interpretation needed for the universal language of love."

I pondered over this when I received it, and I understood it clearly. What is the point of having a godly gift if you use it to make others feel inadequate? If the gift God gave you, namely tongues, is not used as a tool for expressing love, then it defeats the purpose of why it was given to you in the first place. The church has taught me a lot. It has been a playground where I have scraped my knee many a time, but it truly has been my biggest blessing. My life has really been about shifting truths and self-discovery. Church has been the greatest example of how I needed to evaluate and explore my beliefs in order to find the truth, mostly the truth about God, which in turn meant finding the truth about myself.

With regards to the gay community, let us never be an institution where we make people feel less than, where we blame, shame, and hate on others. Our slogan is "Love is love"; let us truly embody this statement. Let us be love, exude love, and share love with the world, unconditionally.

CHAPTER 9

Repression

I AM FEMININE and love being a woman; however, I am attracted to the same. There are three limiting descriptions for the "type" of woman I am/could be:

> **Femme** – (noun & adj) Someone who identifies themselves as feminine, whether it be physically, mentally, or emotionally. Often used to refer to a feminine-presenting queer woman.

> **Lesbian** – (noun) A term used to describe women attracted romantically, erotically, or emotionally to other women.

> **Lipstick Lesbian** – (noun) Usually refers to a lesbian with a feminine gender expression. Can be used in a positive or a derogatory way. Is sometimes also used to refer to a lesbian who is assumed to be (or passes for) straight.

I truly hope that labels will be a thing of the past and that all individuals will be accepted without limiting definitions regarding their pursuit of happiness. I would love to just be me and not have to explain what type of me I am. I am a woman, and I love being one. I love everything about being a woman and have never had any inclination to want to be a man. In my teens, most of my relationships were in secret, both for my partners and myself. I had attempted having boyfriends and had one for a little while whilst I was figuring things out. I cared about him and got on with him so well, but he felt like a mate, and each time he would kiss me, I felt gross and wanted him to stop. I didn't like him in that way.

I tried relationships with boys a few times, but the chemistry was never there. No chemistry, no electricity, no desire, no passion, and certainly no romantic love. I just simply couldn't connect with them that way. Emotionally and sexually, there was nothing there, and I couldn't make it be there. I had crushes on women since I could remember (as early as nine years old), but I ignored them and tried to be "normal." The relationships I had with women were mostly secret. In my teens, we would pretend we were just friends, and most of the times, our parents believed us, so we could go into our bedrooms and kiss. As I reached my twenties, I had more serious relationships and noticed that I dated women similar to me. They were from similar backgrounds and had the same trouble coming out. To me, it was crazy that our parents didn't notice there were never any boys around. I had a lot of male friends also, so maybe it was more difficult for my parents to read the signs.

As I entered my thirties, I began attracting older women. I'm not sure why this happened, as I had friends of all ages. I did, however, prefer conversations with my older friends. One evening, shortly after a particularly destructive relationship, my friends took me out, and I met a girl. She was beautiful, and we started talking; we bought each other drinks, and one thing led to another. We started dating shortly after and couldn't get enough of each other. A month went by, and the relationship deepened. After the second month, however, I noticed she wasn't as available as she had been previously; our conversations had changed. Needless to say, there was reason for concern. I confronted her about it, and she came clean: She was married to a man, and he had returned from a business trip.

I was mortified and broke it off completely, but I was left with questions that needed answering. She said that she married a man to satisfy her family and explained that she could never disgrace her family by openly being who she really was. Life is full of lessons, and this was definitely a big one. I saw my own false and disempowered future if I were I to do the same. She was sorry; I forgave her, but her life haunted me. I wondered if I could do that. Could I live a lie?

Throughout my life, it was as though the few people who knew I was gay spread the word to other people who were interested in me. The only problem with this was that the majority of them were of European background and were stuck in the closet (many were in heterosexual marriages in an attempt to solidify the lie).

Like the sunrise, she demanded my attention. Her eyes seemed to call out to me in her longing for love. "Can you see me?" her eyes whispered.

"I can see how beautiful you are," I would respond telepathically. "Do you see how beautiful you are?"

Tracy was an older woman, almost twenty years my senior, and we had become friends. We met at an awareness seminar and hit it off. We connected well; she told me about her history with men, and I told her about mine with women. We had a lot of the same interests and shared a few mutual friends, and we just enjoyed each other's company. One evening, I received a call from her suggesting we hang out, and I agreed. We decided to watch the next season of *Empire* together and maybe do some painting.

She arrived with a bottle of wine, and I got out a platter of cheese and fresh fruit; we sat and talked for about ten minutes or so. I noticed she wasn't her usual self and felt a wave of discomfort travel through me, not knowing where it was coming from. A few seconds later, she began to undress and asked if she could kiss me. I backed away quickly, said no, and asked her to put her clothes back on.

I didn't know what to do. Do I kick her out of my apartment? But she's naked? So much was going through my mind, and I felt trapped. She kept trying to touch me. I didn't know where to go, and so I put my hands over my head, attempting to stop her from trying to kiss me; she wrapped her legs around me and pleaded that she "needed this."

I asked her again to please stop and put her clothes back on, but she lowered my arms and went in for a kiss. I didn't know what to do to take control of the situation and felt somewhat guilty from the emotional blackmail, and so I let it happen. I was uncomfortable and refused to take my clothes off, despite her repeated attempts to remove them.

It was an awkward situation, and I never expected it from her. She had been married before, to a man, and had always spoken about boyfriends. I forgive her and myself for what happened. I've learnt over time that people who do crazy things like this are acting out of fear and from many years of suppressing their true selves. To me, this situation demonstrated that she had repressed her feelings for so long that she desperately wanted to be with a woman and saw an opportunity through me. I have often found that the more true to myself I am and the more transparent I am, the more I become a mirror to women who are repressing who they truly are.

I have attracted similar situations before, though not as full on as this one, and have tried to understand why. I am an empowered gay woman at this stage of my life, but it seems that my past is still a part of me, and its lessons are reflected in the eyes of those in my life who haven't accepted themselves. I know those eyes, for they were once my own.

If I am at a gathering and there is a woman there who has been questioning her sexuality, it won't take long before she finds her way over to me, wanting to talk about it (or possibly do more than that). My only message to these beautiful souls is that your choices should be completely yours and no one else's. We are here for a very short time. Life is challenging enough without the added burden of denying our own impulses. How can we transcend these impulses if we cannot even acknowledge them? I think sexuality is absolutely beautiful, and yet, somewhere deep within, I can see that it is still only a superficial expression of love. It is not yet divine. I'm not saying that I'm going to be a celibate monk or anything, but I suspect that the reality of who we are is far beyond our sexuality.

"We forget that we are born free; we seem to have forgotten that." – Michael Bernard Beckwith

I love this quote, and as I was listening to Michael's latest book on audio, it moved me to tears. It is absolutely true that we are born free, and we still are free. Michael's interpretation of freedom reminded me of my lifelong friend; we will call her Leanne. Leanne told me one day that although she had a great job and owned a house and had many luxuries, she felt empty. She always wanted to do something meaningful in her life, and she often compared herself to me. She admired my reaching-for-the-stars approach to life; it could be considered irresponsible and crazy to many, but to her, it was admirable. She loved that I wanted my career so bad, I would work two and three jobs for it.

She often said, "At least you are living." She told me she wished she had something to reach for and something that made her want to push harder and live on purpose.

It was hard for me to hear her speak about her own life as meaningless; she meant the world to me. We had been friends since we were children, and I loved her. She was a great friend to me; how could she be meaningless? This situation really upset me, and I told her how I felt in my heart. I said that if all she ever wanted in this life was to be the best friend possible to her friends, she was already achieving a life on purpose. I explained to her that we can all do something. It doesn't matter how big or small; we can always contribute, and we can always serve. The ways in which we serve do not have to be grand or lavish; they can be small gestures, as long as they come from our heart and with pure intention.

I also said that we can achieve this today; we don't have to wait for something to happen, especially with regard to serving, as there are so many people in need, even closer than we could imagine. She was moved by what I said and thought about it deeply. One day, Leanne was watching the local news; there was a family with seven children and one more on the way, and the father had just lost his job. As she watched, her heart bled for this family, and she realised that they were only a few minutes' drive from where she lived.

Without hesitation, she emailed the station and asked for the details of this family so that she could help them out. The station arranged for them to meet, and Leanne told the family that she would support them financially until the husband found another job. She didn't tell anyone what she was doing; she did it in complete secrecy and asked the family to keep it between them. Months later, she confided in me and told me what she was doing; out of tremendous awe, I began to tear up. She explained to me that she followed her heart, and it led her to help this family. Each time she went to give them money, the mother would be silent in awe of what Leanne was doing; the gratitude she felt towards Leanne was expressed in the intensity of her eyes and the continual question: "Why are you helping me?"

Leanne mentioned that the father was very distant at first and didn't know what to make of her; perhaps he felt inferior as he could no longer support his family. Leanne kept the visits short and sweet; the children would be all over her with love and appreciation, not really knowing what she was doing but just showering her with love anyway. Children are beautiful like that; they show love just because. Leanne supported the family for about a year; there were several times on the journey where I was amazed at how my friend had opened her heart and listened to its call. I told her how proud I was of her, and we laughed at how I had told her it could be a small gesture, and she had gone and done something so huge. She told me that it was the best thing she had ever done in her entire life, better than getting a great job, better than owning her own home, and better than any other moment she had ever had.

This act filled her heart beyond measure; one day, when we had gone for one of our usual walks, she said to me, "I now know why we should give." I know this lesson well because as much as I struggle within myself to receive, it is actually so life changing when you give. In fact, when you open your heart to life, the divinity in you wants to pour out blessings on others.

The point of this story is that each moment is an opportunity to decide who we want to be. We can be our true divine selves and live from that space. Today, I am a writer and maybe tomorrow an author. I never knew I would write a book, but here I am today, a writer. It is both interesting and exciting what can happen when we become one with this moment right here and now, trusting in what spirit is guiding us towards. May the divinity in me never stop surprising me with the bliss of life, and may I continue to look at this world through the eyes of love.

I had many spiritual experiences with Leanne. When we met, we instantly clicked as soul sisters. We had a lot in common and were just simply drawn to one another. My friends and my family have always considered me spiritual; I'm not sure why that is or how I got this reputation. When I was a child, the priest would quiz me on the Bible, and I would always know the answer and sometimes offer him insight on the scriptures. I believe I knew the Bible so well because of my near-death experience as a child. In fact, I felt like God had downloaded spiritual insight into me from that experience. In high school, I always got extremely high marks in religious studies; I would often wonder why I couldn't do that with every other subject.

I had not studied much about religion or spirituality at this stage of my life, but for some reason, I would do well with minimal study. I remember one exam, my teacher said to me that he didn't understand much of what I wrote, but he felt like it was accurate and insightful, giving me a A+. Due to this aspect, I found myself attracted to friends who were on spiritual paths also, whether they knew it or not. Many times, friends would seek spiritual counselling from me or ask for prayer; at times, it would make me uncomfortable because I was seeking knowledge from spiritual teachers and gurus myself. Nevertheless, I enjoyed spiritual conversation and never lacked inspiration in this regard; there was always something to talk about when it came to spirit.

Leanne and I frequently went for walks late at night; this coincided with a very intense breakup with her boyfriend. For months, we walked almost every night, even when it rained, and she would vent. She was in the darkest place I had ever seen her, and I was worried. I would let her talk for the first months because I wanted her to release all the poison going on within her and let go of it once and for all, but there came a day when I felt like I had heard it all. I had heard enough. I had heard of the breakup recited over and over, and I decided that this particular night, I was going to do the talking.

I started the conversation with, "Your husband is coming soon. I can feel it."

I don't know what I was thinking, but I knew she wanted a partner, and I know what she wanted him to be like, after many years of her telling me about her dream man.

For the first time in months, Leanne was silent, and I was the one talking. I began telling her a story about what her husband will look and act like, what he will do for a living, and how he would treat her. I made up a story so lovely that anyone would want this man. For the first few walks, she just listened to me; each week, I would add new character traits. I would talk about the nice things he would do for her and so on.

A month or so into my story, Leanne began to add elements to this made-up man as well, and more importantly, she began to smile again, and that made me happy. I felt that there was progress, and it wasn't all doom and gloom. We spoke about him as if he were real; some nights, we laughed about how amazing we had created him. There were times she would also add in what she would be like with this man, how she would behave or change, what she would and would not accept, and so on.

Months went by, and our walks became enjoyable again. We would talk and laugh, and I felt like I had my friend back. Three months after our conversations about this imaginary man, he appeared. They courted for a couple of months, which was strange for both of them, as they each had the habit of jumping into relationships. Due to the fact that they had both suffered bad breakups, they took it slow.

On our walks, she would tell me what this man was like; much to our surprise, he was everything we had spoken about: to the last detail. We had spoken about how he was sensitive and spiritual but also a manly man, and he was exactly that. We had spoken about how he was traditional and came from the same background as her, and he was exactly that. He was the exact height and had the exact personality; he was the exact description of the man we had imagined. We had spoken about how he was athletic and how they loved doing physical activities together. He was everything we had asked for. When I met him and had a chance to speak to him and get to know him a little, I could not believe my eyes; standing before me was the man we had asked for. Years have passed, and they are together and truly happy, a match made in heaven.

I share this story with single friends and also use this principle for myself. I have had "dream boards" of my ideal partner and have encouraged my friends to do the same. One of my friends and I did one, but it wasn't happening for us; in frustration, she asked me one day, "Why isn't this occurring for us?"

To be honest, I had wondered this myself, so I asked the same question in a meditation, and the answer I received, as always, astounded me. Leanne was committed to her vision; she *knew* who she wanted. She also sacrificed elements of herself to be with him. I need to explain this further, and of course, this isn't for everyone. She had prayed to God after she had met her partner, and in gratitude, she thanked God and told him that she would honour this man and this relationship and treat it as sacred. This says a lot about her spiritual growth, and I am so proud of her. In receiving what she had prayed for, her first instinct was to offer gratitude. She treated this relationship like a sacred gift from God and cherished it. She taught me a lot about life and relationships.

This reminded me of a moment I had with my spiritual teacher. It was her birthday, and I bought her a gift; upon receiving the gift, she said to me, "You are my gift." Leanne reminded me of this moment, that we are all gifts to this planet and to one another. May we all treat each other in this way: as sacred gifts from God.

CHAPTER 10

Believe in Miracles

HAVING TWO NEAR-DEATH experiences and returning to tell the story is a miracle in itself. I believe in miracles and have experienced them first-hand. It is through these seemingly greater miracles that I am able to perceive the more subtle miracles: a sunrise, a gentle breeze, a helping hand, or a moment of joy. All of life is a miracle if we choose to see it that way. My near-death experiences definitely had a great influence on shaping the person I am today.

My first NDE occurred at the age of six while being molested by my next-door neighbour. My spirit left my body, and I remember that all pain, suffering, and bad feelings stayed with my body, as I rose from the cage of the body with a feeling of peace and elation. Absolute bliss. Experience on a higher plane of existence is very difficult to comprehend. It's possible that our mind creates symbols that are relatable or relevant to us. I grew up a Catholic, so Jesus was my chaperone on the higher planes.

I believe we have two minds, in a way. We have our permanent mind (or our soul's mind), and we have our temporary mind (or physical mind). Our physical mind is analytical in its cognitive functions, whilst our soul's mind is intuitive in its functions of feeling and awareness. Miracles are perceived through our souls mind: the mind that is *not* concerned with data collection, evaluation, analysis, labelling, and categorising but is instead concerned with how things feel and our place in this mysterious and ineffable universe.

Aside from my own experiences, I have also witnessed many other miracles in church. As you can surely tell by now, my experiences in church have been interesting, to say the least, with experiences on both ends of the spectrum. I honour churches and temples, as I believe they are sacred and built as sanctuaries for surrendering to God. These places are special and should be honoured greatly. I have often said it's the people in them, myself included, who are contaminated with judgements and distortions. The fact remains, I have witnessed many miracles at church. I have seen people get out of wheelchairs, cancer has been cured, broken hearts have been restored, and blind people regained their sight. It is my belief that our permanent self is whole in truth, and healing is the removal of self-imposed limitations and distortions (our temporary self expands to contain more of our permanent self). God wants us healed and whole, but the decision to actually heal is always our own. The power of surrendering to a higher power is indisputable.

Even the universally successful twelve-step program is founded on surrendering to a higher power. This is because we don't really know what it is we actually want. By surrendering to a higher power, we are activating a part of self that can project past our pain, confusion, desires, and fears and make the decision to let go of all that does not serve us. Healing is the removal of layers of illusion to reveal the wholeness that we are. With just a little willingness to surrender our lives to God/divine love/the universe, we are immediately supported, as though all of heaven has been waiting for this willingness. Preachers, priests, and spiritual healers do not have more power than we do; they simply have a greater willingness to surrender to a higher power.

Through my obvious confusion, I was convinced that my

sexuality needed to be "healed." During this time of trying to heal my sexuality, I went to see many international superstar preachers. I not only attended in the audience, I made sure I got close enough to receive a healing. I met most of the big-time preachers you see on TV, shook their hands, and in desperation, asked for a healing. I was getting desperate and figured maybe I need to have a word with the best of them, so I pushed my way through crowds just to get to them and demand their attention in order to heal my "illness."

With the exception of one preacher, none had any answers for me. I will never forget meeting one of my favourite American preachers. I was so excited to see him; I loved his sense of humour and his enormous heart. You could tell he just loved people, and people loved him dearly. He never asked for money from his audience and never made people feel unwelcome; to me, he was a true representative of Jesus.

I managed to speak to him after his service in Sydney in a completely jam-packed stadium. I asked him to help me. He responded, "I can't help anyone, but the God in me and you can. What's wrong, girl?" He spoke in a strong Louisiana accent.

His energy was so lively, and while gazing at his big smile, I found myself smiling also and remembered what I wanted to ask him: "Can you help me stop being gay?"

His demeanour changed, and I could see that he could feel my pain. I expected that he would pray for me or maybe exorcise the demon or something, but he said, "God is very much a part of you, as he is everybody else; don't ever let anyone tell you different. I'm not going to pray for a healing of your sexuality. I am going to pray that God guides you to wholeness and he shows you his unconditional love and acceptance every day and guides you to your life purpose. People may not accept us, but God accepts us because he created us all with his own hands. You want to see God's glory, young lady? Look in the mirror; you're his greatest masterpiece."

He was exactly as I'd imagined him to be, only better. He handled my situation with love, compassion, and incredible wisdom. I'll never forget his words and how gracious he was with me. Sexuality is such a hard subject for preachers to handle, but this man of God seemed to understand that homosexuality is completely natural and does not require healing.

Although I have met some good preachers, many of them had beliefs on the subject of sexuality that were quite narrow. It is evident in the fact that homosexuals cannot be leaders or participate in activities at church; we have many limitations and are barely allowed to attend. I used to laugh when they would say that church is for everyone because for homosexuals or people who made them feel uncomfortable, that welcome message was short-lived. It wouldn't be long before they would be approaching you with questions on whether you are an active homosexual and if you've ever considered Christian therapies like ex-gay ministries.

One of the greatest miracles I am experiencing now is that the ex-gay ministry program that I completed is now closed and inactive. Many large corporations supporting ex gay therapies have shut their doors. Miracles do happen. My mum would confront me occasionally on the subject of sexuality, and I would kindly remind her that if the Catholic church didn't let up on women, she would not have the role she has now, and that if the churches didn't let up on divorced people, the churches would be empty. We forget that not too long ago, people weren't allowed to attend church for the colour of their skin. Thank God for the miracles that happen daily, showing us the error of our ways.

Many times in my life, I have thought about miracles. A miracle is communication with God. A miracle is the awareness of truth in a world of illusions. A miracle, contrary to its connotations, is the most natural thing in this world. It is our distorted perceptions and limited ideas of ourselves that is unnatural, and yet these distortions and limitations are so profound and deeply founded that to be aware of truth is a miracle. To one person, a miracle could be getting a dream job, waking up in the morning grateful for the sun's rays, watching a flower bloom, an answered prayer, an impossible circumstance overcome, a moment of forgiveness.

I remember specifically asking the universe for a job that paid double and was half the work, and a week later, I got it and resigned from my existing job. After working a few months in my new role, I prayed that I had even more time to do the things I really wanted to and had been putting off. The very next week, I was accused of something I didn't do at work and was asked to leave while they conducted an investigation. Both wishes were granted, in very different ways. Whilst I waited for the investigation to conclude, I meditated a lot, went for long walks, did things I had been putting off, and whilst doing all this, I prayed for the miracle of my vindication. As this all happened, I was able to analyse this situation from several perspectives and learnt a thing or two about miracles.

Miracles are what we need most, the shedding of our fears and illusions, opening up to love, and growing into who we really are. We may have our own specific ideas about what that looks like, but we are often wrong. Miracles are about elevating our faith as we start to recognise that God knows what we need, but we may not. As worried and anxious as I was waiting for my prayer to be answered, hoping that everything at work would be okay, I knew deep inside that in God's hands, everything is always okay, regardless of the outcome. This is my faith.

"God calls and you do not hear because you are preoccupied with your own voice." – *A Course in Miracles*.

A Course in Miracles is a holy scripture; this is one of my favourite verses from it. God is constantly speaking to us, but we often cannot hear his voice when it calls from an unexpected place. I met an astrologer at my café, and we became friends. Our conversations were fascinating. He and his wife invited me over to his place so that he could show me all his telescopes and his studio. I walked into the most incredible studio I'd ever seen. He had a Bible dating back to the early 1700s. He had ancient books on philosophy and religion as well as tons of books on astrology and astronomy.

His first question was, "Do you want to see what the earth looked like on your arrival here?"

To which I replied, "Absolutely," in a heartbeat.

I'll never forget this experience. After showing me my chart, he explained that the earth, universe, and God never stop moving, never stop creating, and never stop communicating; when it is our turn to embark on this journey of life, it is as if we jump onto an already moving roller coaster of life. Life, the universe, the earth never stop; they are always active. After explaining a bit about how the universe works from a very technical perspective, he read my chart. Without knowing much about me from our limited conversations, he was able to tell me about my cycles of life and my personality and what makes me a Libra star sign. Although he blew me away with his accuracy, he also asked very politely and carefully about my sexuality.

I told him the truth, and he responded, "Take a look at this," and to my surprise, when it came to relationships and romance, there was a female symbol on my chart.

Coincidence maybe, but the details of my life and personality were too accurate for him to have guessed. When I arrived home in the early hours of the morning, I was exhausted and yet driven to keep learning and thinking about everything we discussed. I wondered about God, the universe, and my place within it all. Everything in creation is a miracle. We are walking miracles and have the shared nature of our creator to perform miracles. We often relate miracles to manifestations of healing or wishes that come true, but life itself is a grand miracle. When the astrologer referred to the fact that the entire universe, God, and the earth are always communicating, it got me thinking about whether we truly listen, and how often we ignore what we have heard. If God is a radio station that is constantly on air, how often do we tune in (and not just during a hardship, where we need the miracle yesterday). If we were always tuned in, we wouldn't need to pray in such a way because we would already be in direct communication. The story of Job describes that in our slumber, God seals our instructions. Even in our sleep, God is talking to us.

When I was younger, I had profound encounters with the voice of God while playing soccer. In fact, sometimes God would speak to me so much on the soccer field, I would get distracted. It became evident to me when other teammates noticed and asked me to pray before our games.

I was put on the spot and felt a bit embarrassed; most importantly, I didn't want to sound like a preacher, and so my prayers went a little like this: "God, I ask that you keep everyone on the team free of injury. I pray for a fair game from the players and also the referees. I pray that you would help us with our egos if we lose," and then to make them all laugh, I would finish with, "And please control my mum and dad on the sidelines and stop them from embarrassing me and the team. Thank you, and amen."

Taking a moment together to be aware of God completely changed the atmosphere, and the times that we didn't, something always went horribly wrong (or at the very least, we lost our focus). One year in particular, I sensed the team was feeling that I was a bit of a ball hog (which was true). I wanted to score the goals, and I wanted the glory. God put it in my heart to pass the ball as much as I could; I was hesitant but decided to listen. Not only did we play better that season, but I was leading goal scorer, and our general goal tally was up by more than 50 percent from last season. People were scoring more goals because I was passing the ball more, but the amazing thing was that my tally didn't drop; in fact, it increased.

There was another soccer experience that I can't leave out because it's the dearest one to my heart. My first soccer team was a group of amateurs, myself included, and the father of one of the girls had played for an international league, and so he instantly became the coach. He was an amazing coach and an even more amazing player. We learnt so much from him. The season was hard, and we lost every game. We were so discouraged, but each week, we got better and better. We were up against the toughest teams, and when you play with people who are better than you, you always become better.

It was the last game of the season, and we had come so far in skill and as a team. We didn't expect to win, but we hoped for at least a goal to give us momentum for the next season. I got the ball and started running towards goal; my sister was in a better position to score, and I heard a voice tell me to pass it to her. She kicked the ball off my pass, and it was a beautiful play. The ball looked like it was going in, but the goalkeeper managed to push it out wide.

We were so disappointed; my sister had tears in her eyes. I told her not to worry and assured her that we would get another chance before the end of the game. I noticed that with disappointment came an intense hunger; my entire team was now buzzing with the anticipation of what it would be like to score; all of a sudden, they wanted it more than anything. My sister was probably the most hungry for a goal now. Sure enough, a few minutes later, she delivered me an amazing cross, and off a volley, I smashed the ball as hard as I could. There was absolute silence throughout the entire stadium, and then my family, friends, and teammates yelled in unison at the top of their lungs: Goal!

It almost didn't seem real until I was embraced by my team from all angles in a wild celebration. My sister was elated, and it was honestly one of the most memorable moments of my life. I learnt so much from experiences such as these. It is so much better to give than receive because giving *is* receiving. I gave up an opportunity to score to let my sister have the glory, and I ended up realising that the glory was ours collectively. The energy of the entire team scored that goal, not just me. Playing soccer taught me a lot about life and the importance of unity. In a team sport, you often have to try and function as one: read each other, work with one another, sense one another, and help one another. It's a beautiful demonstration of how life works too. The more we work as one, the better the results. When our function includes those around us, our identity expands beyond our finite self and grows into the broader identity of the collective Sonship of God. This is oneness.

My prayers these days are less "Please, God, help" or "Please, God, I need this" and more "Speak to me" and "What do I need to know?" and "How can I serve better, love better?" The church focuses a lot on prayer, but the Bible speaks a lot about meditation. Abraham, Moses, David, Solomon, and Jesus spent much time in reflection and meditation. The Bible is full of stories where people needed to leave society in order to be alone with God. David in particular is one of my favourite people of the Old Testament. Apart from his incredible story, he also wrote the psalms, which along with Proverbs is one of my favourite books of the Bible.

Psalm 23
A Psalm of David

The LORD is my shepherd, I lack nothing.
He makes me lie down in green pastures,
he leads me beside quiet waters,
he refreshes my soul.
He guides me along the right paths
for his name's sake.
Even though I walk
through the darkest valley,
I will fear no evil,
for you are with me;
your rod and your staff,
they comfort me.

You prepare a table before me
in the presence of my enemies.
You anoint my head with oil;
my cup overflows.

Surely your goodness and love will follow me
all the days of my life,
and I will dwell in the house of the LORD
forever.

This famous psalm of David was written after he had a man killed purely because he wanted his wife, Bathsheba. He was the king, and so he ordered her husband be put in the front line of battle so he could be with his wife, as he had already got her pregnant. Although they were in love, in one of his meditations, he was told that he had done the wrong thing, and at the same time, the Prophet Samuel came to tell him as well. It was almost as though David ignored God, and so God sent a physical messenger who told him that the consequence (not punishment) for his murder would be that they would lose their first son. It was his first lesson of karma, and it was shown to him that he had put this on himself. In this time, he fasted and meditated and then wrote a psalm that would be remembered for all time.

David wanted a miracle that he knew he could not receive. Often in life, we expect a miracle to serve our fragmented, temporary self when it can only serve our permanent self. A miracle will never take us further into the depths of illusion and despair but instead will lead us to the kingdom of heaven, to love. Would we want anything less from what we have termed a miracle? David took something that was precious to someone, and then life took something that was precious to him. We reap what we sow. If we didn't know what loss felt like, then it's understandable we would continue to take from others. Life teaches us the lessons we must learn; the miracle is that the voice of God uses all of creation for the lessons. We must learn to hear the voice of God in all things to allow miracles to teach us who we are.

It is my deepest belief that true miracles all stem from love. I have often wondered about the function of a miracle and can only perceive it through what I feel in my personal experiences. When I was ill and had my near-death experience, there was an incredible amount of love around me. My parents wanted me to live, my sisters wanted me home, and my extended family and friends were all praying and hoping that I would be okay. They were doing that because of the love they felt for me. There is nothing that separates me from anyone else, so why was I blessed with the miracle of healing when so many others continue to suffer in illness?

I know just how blessed I am to have experienced such a miracle and can see that it was the result of an incredible amount of love that surrounded me (and surrounds me still). I received more insight into this when I read about when Jesus healed a man who had been blind since birth. The people around Jesus were asking him why he was born blind. They asked if it was the parents' fault for their sins or just plain bad luck, to which Jesus replied, "Nothing is a mistake and nothing happens by chance; this man's purpose was to be a demonstration to the world of the power of God."

Jesus continued by placing some clay on the man's eyes and told him to go to the river to wash it off. After following Jesus' instructions, he was no longer blind. I found this story fascinating because I believe it tells us that all of our shortcomings, our disabilities, our failures, and our mistakes can (and should) become demonstrations of the miraculous work of God. Through miracles, we finally see what God knows we deserve, in contrast to what we think we deserve. This is what I choose to believe about my life; what has transpired in my life is not a curse or a failure, but an opportunity to reveal the divine nature of God within me to surpass it all and turn it into something great. Something miraculous.

CHAPTER 11

Self-Acceptance

To say that I have achieved complete acceptance of myself and abolished all the negativity in my life would not be accurate. There are brief moments when this is true, but like everything of this world, the knowing is impermanent. I believe that we have lost our true self; the journey of remembering who we truly are, as God created us, is a lifelong process (it may even take many lives). It took a great deal of habitual negative thinking and energy over a period of thirty-three years to create the belief that I was ill and broken, so it seems silly to think I could completely redefine my idea of self without the same amount of habitual positive thinking and energy.

Awakening to self begins with awareness, though it often takes some time and energy to retrain our mind and heart in redirecting our thoughts and emotions from fear to love. Habits must be changed, negativity must be released, and forgiveness of self and others needs to unfold. For most of us, healing is a process and cannot all be done at once. This process is often painful. I have learnt that there is also a beauty within the pain we experience, which the Bible refers to as the beauty for ashes. It is beautiful because our true self has always been (and will always be) perfect in eternity, while our self-created self seems to suffer still in its own illusions. It is beautiful because we are safe, and we always will be safe.

You have heard it said that it doesn't matter what others think of you, only what you think and feel about yourself. How could this be useful if your current idea of self is distorted? There is truly great power in surrendering our thoughts, emotions, and ideas to a higher power, whether you call it the Holy Spirit, the universe, or the great spaghetti monster. Carl Jung called it "Spiritum" throughout his contributions to the universally successful twelve-step program. I have learnt to filter my thoughts and feelings through spirit. We feel terrible when something bad is happening, but we rarely view it from a higher perspective whilst it's happening. There is only one perspective I am interested in, and I have learnt that for me, it is the only one that matters. How does God see me? How does God see my brothers and sisters? How does the divine that lives within me see us all? That is the only perspective I am interested in now.

I allowed the thoughts and feelings of others to influence how I felt about myself for thirty-three years. People often call me gullible, and although it is a Libra trait, I don't believe that I am. I choose to see only good in people. This is what it means to see people for who they truly are: their soul. We are all good at our core because we were created by love. Everything else is our own creation and a distortion of the truth. I do not see myself as perfect (in fact, quite the opposite). This reveals to me that I still have a lot of work to do before understanding my true self. I'm a faster learner when it comes to seeing others as they truly are, and I have learnt to really see people for their soul, their divine self.

I guess it doesn't really matter whether I learn to love myself first or my brothers and sisters, for we are the same to God. When we can truly see each other, we become the sun and shine our light in all its glory so that we may both know what we are. When we look to the side, we may darkness but know that it cannot be so, for the light in front of us is what we really are. In the light of truth, we are all perfect creations of God, with self-made shadows behind us. The shadows are behind us because as humans, we are always striving to be better than we used to be; there is something within that drives us towards the light, no matter how dark the paths we have walked.

True acceptance is to see ourselves in the light of love. If we could see ourselves in this light, we would be so at peace that we would only seek to share this feeling with others. We would truly see others if we could only see ourselves. Loving myself has been a challenge; for many years, I felt unlovable. There is a stigma attached to sexual abuse and sexuality that presents an element of segregation. Sexual abuse victims are often treated as though they are no longer worthy of real love, as they are damaged goods, when real love is all they crave. They spend the rest of their lives trying to find it. We look everywhere in search of it, and when it continues to elude us, we find empty replacements, mirages of love. They appear to be real, but they are not. Not even close.

Self-acceptance has a lot to do with our wounding; there have been many times I have looked in the mirror and could visibly see the wounds I carry. I have seen them in my weight, in my smile (or lack thereof), in my expression, and in my eyes. The eyes are truly the windows to the soul. My mother always said that whenever I cried, I could make the world cry with me. I wasn't sure what she meant by that, thinking she was saying it just because she's my mum and loves me and hates seeing me cry. As I got older and witnessed myself cry in front of a mirror, I saw what she meant. Each tear is a wound speaking of its need for release; the redness in the eye is the pressure required on the body to let go and surrender; and the glaze is a portal opening to allow for more light to come in and out.

I believe that part of my journey towards self-acceptance has been about seeing beyond the wounds, beyond the scarring, and rediscovering my divine self, as God sees me. Through the eyes of God, I see myself a victor, not a victim. I am a warrior, not a wimp. I am abundantly blessed and have never been cursed. I am not my story, and I am not my scars. I am a conqueror of darkness and not just its weary survivor. When we can look up and say thank you for the journey, all of it, we are on our way to self-acceptance. We are remembering who we are.

Moving towards complete self-acceptance appears to involve the surrender and release of our past and what is yet to come. This seemingly difficult task is achieved simply by accepting it all as it is in the present moment: seeing ourselves as we truly are, accepting our identity as love, and surrendering all the rest. For me, Christ is the perfect embodiment of this level of acceptance and love. He loved what the world deemed unlovable and unacceptable because he knew what we truly are and refused to believe in our self-made illusions.

God is truly the reason I am alive today. He is the reason I got through it all and survived. One of my favourite quotes is "Man should be ashamed to die without contributing to the betterment of mankind." I feel that there is such waste in giving up but great reward in persevering. I am a living example of the rewards of perseverance. I don't want to leave this life without contributing to the betterment, of mankind. I'm beginning to see that there is no greater way of achieving this than by becoming (or remembering) the best version of myself.

This is what Gandhi meant when he said, "Be the change you wish to see in the world." I have accepted that this is what I came to this earth to learn. I am not a mistake made by God. I am actually his perfect glory, his masterpiece, his divine creation. I remember my first realisation of this. I had a *Bruce Almighty* moment when for the first time, I saw myself through the eyes of God. It was the first time I had ever expressed an ounce of love toward myself.

Continual self-love and self-acceptance seem to be a difficult and cyclical process. I don't often love myself. Most of us don't love ourselves the way we should. I struggle with self-love; this has been the hardest chapter to articulate because I promised myself I would keep this book raw and honest. I am learning to love myself enough to allow love to flow through me into others. Love is the only thing in this world that multiplies when it is shared. We have the deeply rooted idea that when we give, we lose something, and when receive, someone else must lose. The more we love ourselves, the more we bless others with our love, and the more we love others, the more we bless ourselves; it's as simple as that.

I've decided to bless people with my love, but if that love isn't coming from the right place, then it won't really be a blessing to anyone and certainly not to myself, either. Is this love? It's an interesting thought: blessing someone with your love. It makes you think about whether love is truly love when it is given sacrificially, to your detriment. You can't rob Peter to pay Paul. So if it does not multiply when shared, it is not love. If it doesn't extend peace to all it touches, it's a distorted version of love. There is no reciprocity in love because love is what we truly are.

One question I have asked myself a lot is how to love the aspects of myself that are so despised by those around me. I could spout clichés like "One day at a time," and that would be true to a degree, but the more helpful answer is that I stopped hearing the voices that told me who I was and began telling myself a new story about who I am. I told myself I am lovable, I am not sick, I am perfect health, I am not ashamed, I have nothing to be ashamed about, I am divine, and I am unique. My uniqueness is my blessing.

A large part of the healing is also to see past the distortions in those who gave you your old story, for they are as perfect in truth as you are. I have started to believe my new story more and more each day, one day at a time. There are still days that I hate myself, but then I remember who told me that I should hate myself and why they told me that story. I remember that I no longer live from that place of fear. I send love to those who sought to turn something beautiful into something ugly, and I remember how beautiful we all are. Anything that tells you that you are inadequate is a distortion of this true beauty. I am hopeful that in being myself, the truest self I can possibly be, this is all people will ever see: simply me.

There is a light in you which cannot die; whose presence is so holy that the world is sanctified because of you. All things that live bring gifts to you, and offer them in gratitude and gladness at your feet. The light in you is what the universe longs to behold. All living things are still before you, for they recognize Who walks with you. The light you carry is their own. – *A Course in Miracles*

Have patience with all things but first with yourself. Never confuse your mistakes with your value as a human being. You're a perfectly valuable, creative, worthwhile person simply because you exist. And no amount of triumphs or tribulations can ever change that. Unconditional self-acceptance is the core of a peaceful mind. – St. Francis of Sales

Having been through some dark times in my life, I feel it is necessary to touch on the ugliness that comes from such events. All of us suffer independently and uniquely, according to our own mental and emotional predispositions. There have been many times in my life when I have felt completely healed and times when I have felt like I haven't gotten much farther than rock bottom. For me, this had a lot to do with self-acceptance. Dealing with the ugliness that comes from dark places and experiences can be tricky.

As fate would have it, I relived a moment of darkness whilst writing this chapter; it was a reminder of the ugliness that can linger if its darkness is not addressed and surrendered into light. Dark experiences such as rape, illness, and rejection can severely alter the ways in which one views and processes the world.

I cannot pretend I am completely free from my past. I still carry much of it with me. There are days when all the issues of my world compound, and I am weak just thinking about the ugliness that was suffered. This affects the way I react to certain people and situations as an adult. Physical scars do not heal immediately, and neither do mental, emotional, or spiritual ones. The deeper the wound, the longer the process of healing.

The same goes for our reactions, which are based on past wounding. As Vipassana teaches, a weak reaction that can easily be reprogrammed is like a line drawn in the sand on a beach. By nightfall, the ocean will have washed it away. Other reactions that are based on deep wounding are like a line etched deep into stone. These reactions are much harder to reprogram and require a great amount of constant awareness and acceptance in order to shift the perspective of its core wounding.

After truly accepting what has become a part of your story, how can you then accept your reactions that are influenced by the perceived "injustice" of this story? If you have truly accepted your story, it will no longer be perceived as an injustice and will not warrant a negative reaction when the wound triggers appear. Our past experiences and our reactions are simply cause and effect. Recognising the effect and desiring to change it is part of the healing process, moving towards acceptance.

With circumstances such as rape, it's difficult to remove the ugliness; I have struggled with this since it happened. The after-effects included no self-worth, destructive behavior and habits, the inability to trust anyone (including myself), and self-hatred, just to name a few. One of my struggles as an adult is the desire to be alone and then, ironically, the sadness of feeling alone. A preacher once told me that loneliness was the absence of purpose, not the absence of people. This made sense to me, as I have always had so many people around me, with such big family and all, so I have no reason to feel alone, but loneliness really has nothing to do with the number of people around you.

For me, the loneliness was much deeper. For most of us, our sense of purpose is cultivated by our involvement with family, friends, and the broader community. People who have faced abuse at a young age often miss out on this important phase of development because our experiences are so different. Often, we are left on the outskirts of society to cultivate our own broken sense of belonging on our own. I never felt like I belonged. Growing up in the church emphasised this feeling even more, and considering I wasn't allowed to have a purpose within the church because of my sexuality, I felt doomed.

We all have a purpose, no matter who we are or what we do. Our highest purpose is divine love, love that transcends identity, culture, sexuality, values, beliefs, and ideas. I wonder how the world would function if we had the courage to share our perceived ugliness unashamed? Most of the ugliness in life, especially the type attached to rape, involves shame. When we react with ugliness, we generally hide it in shame. Over the years, I have had the privilege of sharing stories with other survivors of abuse. I have felt their pain and have seen how they chose to deal with that pain, whether it be self-abuse, allowing others to abuse them, self-mutilation, self-harm, drug abuse, and so on. I am no exception to this and have had my own negative experiences of dealing with my pain. God, meditation, self-observation and reprogramming, spiritual counselling, taking it one day at a time, and bringing myself to the present moment helped me deal with and overcome my reactions of pain.

I have also come to accept this part of myself for exactly what it is, as it is. You've heard it said that our choices are okay as long as you're not hurting anyone, but the reality is that a reaction to pain always hurts someone; often, it is ourselves. Earlier on, I spoke about a woman who came on to me quite forcefully, and I felt violated. After this happened, I found myself pretending that it was no big deal. I swept it under the carpet. My emotions were screaming out for acknowledgement, but I was doing everything I could to forget and move forward. All I knew was that I never wanted to see or hear from her again.

A month later, I woke up at 3 a.m., having an anxiety attack and struggling to breathe. I paced my apartment, thinking about what had happened and why I was experiencing so much anxiety. As I sat disorientated on the couch, my cat seemed to feel my sadness. He climbed onto my shoulders and cuddled into my neck, as I held him gently and kissed him on the head. As he was comforting me, I remember thinking how afraid I am of people and how grateful I was that my cat was there. Animals have an incredible capacity for unconditional love. The anxiety attack was the result of sweeping my emotions under the carpet. If we suppress our emotions, they will only rise again at a later time. We must develop the awareness to perceive our wounding and the forgiveness to heal them.

Meditation plays a big part in my life now. I have meditations that are unforgettable; the memory of them will linger with me for days and sometimes weeks. It's the only time when this chaotic world makes perfect sense.

I want to close this chapter on a meditation I had that was all about self-acceptance. One particular morning, I was in a terrible mood. I was angry, frustrated, and extremely sad. During this time, my boss was giving me grief, even on my days off, and I was still being harassed by the woman who forced herself on me. It was all a little overwhelming. In preparation for my meditation, I sat quietly and put on a beautiful song about love and being in a place of peace. The singer was Jai Jagdeesh (I recommend her for meditations; she is fantastic. I would describe her as a modern-day Enya. Her music has a way of calming and healing you.). After Jai's song "In Dreams," I then listened to the Moses Code. I meditated for forty-five minutes and received the most beautiful revelations on why I was feeling so sad and what it is that I truly desire from life.

Sometimes, things don't work in life because it isn't what you truly want, and you just don't have the guts to admit it or the courage to go for it. I was transported back to my childhood and forward to my future; visions of both were coming and going. It was as though my higher self was telling me that this is what I want (future) and this is why I want it (past).

I remembered drawing a lot as a child and dreaming of different ways to design a jacket or a pair of pants. My visions were telling me that this is what I've always wanted for a career since I was a child; somewhere along the line, I ran into a few dream killers. We all have them; they are not bad people. My family wants nothing more for me than to succeed in my dreams, but they are equally afraid of what might happen if I do not succeed. Big dreams are sometimes difficult to process and envision when your goal is to be the next Oprah, Cindy Crawford, Bill Gates, or Donatella Versace, but our dreams are our dreams, and my dream was to be like Versace.

I wanted my own label, my own studio, and I wanted my own runway shows at fashion weeks around the world. It's a big dream, it's a long shot, and it may seem impossible, but it's my dream. I've wanted this all my life. I don't know why exactly, but I know that in moving away from my dream, I am never totally at peace. I am never fully alive, and I am never completely happy. When I try to live day by day, doing something other than what I feel called to do, I don't feel like I am in the flow of my heart, and the situations around me demonstrate that. Things never go right at work when I am in the wrong occupation. I understand we all need to put food on the table, but I also need to sleep well at night, knowing that I'm honouring my heart's calling and being true to myself.

During the meditation, I was transported to my own future studio in Sydney, and as I walked through the beautiful glass doors, I saw a stunning marble desk in the shape of the infinity symbol. It was big and extravagant and made the entrance grand. I had a receptionist (go figure). There was a magnificent showing space with racks of my clothes (pieces I hadn't created yet). I saw a manufacturing room, and it all seemed so real, as though this was my life. I also saw myself in my home with my friends, some of whom I had not met yet. Their company felt wonderful. My home was in a location I have never thought about living in.

I am so grateful to have had a glimpse into my future and what it is that I truly want. I don't want to be a designer for the fame, fortune, or glamour that comes with this industry; people who know me would know that the business side of it isn't me. I want to be a designer because I love creating. I love designing new ideas and concepts for how we wear items of clothing, changing fastenings, changing the linings and fabrics, using old tailoring techniques to obtain certain looks, and using unique ideas to change the styles. For example, I designed a shirt back in 2002 that had suspenders sewn in an interesting way. A few years later, a famous designer had designed something similar, and it was on the cover of *Vogue*.

These revealing coincidences happen to me often. Designing, for me, is an endless joy. I have drawn for hours on end and can keep going, as the ideas keep flowing. The fact that I don't work in this industry full time is because of the fear I have of living without the security I have now. I have always been too afraid of throwing myself into fashion wholeheartedly; it's probably because I don't feel I fit into that world, either. I'm not underweight, I'm not as attractive as people in this industry, I don't necessarily like to dress up all the time; in fact, I live in Lorna Jane tracksuits. In general, I don't fit the stereotype of a designer, either. I design because I love to create, not because I like to be in the spotlight.

When I had the opportunity to show my designs in New York, it was a very overwhelming opportunity and one I believe I wasn't ready for. It was a taste of what it could be like in the fashion industry. I had to walk out on stage after the show, and I was the most nervous I have ever been in my life. I was so scared. I can still feel the tingles of nervousness, just thinking about that moment. What I cherished from that experience were the people who loved a jacket or a pair of pants, the industry people I made friends with, and the moments I was able to see my designs on display, with lights shining on them.

I also made friends with an amazing girl who modeled in the show and wore one of my outfits. She herself didn't feel she fit in as a model; she didn't really like the attention, but her height, figure, and beautiful face led her to the opportunity, and the industry gravitated towards her. I needed a model for a shoot, and after chatting for a while, she offered to do it for free. We have remained friends, and I'll never forget her generosity and how we connected by sharing the same feeling on opposite ends of the runway.

I discovered a lot about self-acceptance during meditation that day. God, spirit, or the universe knows exactly what we need for our growth and highest good. Like a gentle current, everything in our life is leading us to where we need to be. We often swim against this current, holding onto our own distorted ideas, fears, and expectations. Self-acceptance has a lot to do with surrender, trusting that all we need to do is follow our heart and remain in the flow of its loving wisdom, allowing the current to take us to who we really are.

What we do for a living is not who we are, but it is where we spend most of our time and energy. It is where most of us find purpose, and it is where we create. Would it not then be wise to make sure it's in line with our hearts? I have no regrets because I don't find living in the past very helpful. Instead, I choose to focus on what I can do now to change the future and to make it one that truly resonates with my heart. One of the human desires we all carry deep within our souls is that of significance and legacy. What are we doing that is significant within this world, and what legacy are we leaving behind once we are no longer here? What are we passing on to the people we leave behind? Have we fulfilled our calling?

Meditation has a way of putting everything into perspective. We are so consumed with our external world and pay little attention to our internal world. The irony is that our external world is a reflection of our thoughts, emotions, values, ideas, and beliefs (i.e., our internal world). We are constantly creating our reality, whether consciously or unconsciously. Wouldn't you rather create it consciously?

Through meditation, I was able to realise my own potential and develop the courage to follow. We must follow our joy, our excitement, and our peace. God, spirit, or the universe speaks to us through everything, even our emotions. What better sign do you need than boredom or depression to know you are not following your heart? What better sign than joy or excitement to know that you are? With all my heart, I believe in this dream because I believe in myself. While working as a chef in a small country town, I received an invitation to New York Fashion Week to present my designs. If that wasn't enough of a sign, I don't know what is.

"Owning our story and loving ourselves through that process is the bravest thing we'll every do." – Brene Brown

I believe that God, spirit, or the universe does conspire to make your dreams a reality; I very much believe in the law of attraction. I also believe that until we accept ourselves and transcend our story, the universe cannot help us grow because we are not actually asking for growth. The universe doesn't understand hollow affirmations or meaningless words. It understands energy. If the energy you are putting out is that of a victim, powerless in a frightening world where things just seem to happen to you, the universe will keep providing similar situations of the same vibration until you can learn what is required.

If the energy you are putting out is that of an empowered, successful being who is consciously creating a reality of love, the universe will bring about people and circumstances that match this higher vibration. With clear intention and with our hearts as the guiding force behind our choices, absolutely anything is possible. Meditation has helped me on my journey of self-acceptance as I begin to understand that I am divine love. Everything else is my own creation and a distortion of the truth.

During my NDE, while walking with Christ, I noticed that he wasn't just looking at me; he was experiencing all of me, and I knew in that moment how much he loves me: all of me. Seeing myself through

Jesus' eyes, I was able to truly love myself, knowing that love is my true identity, beyond the mind and emotion, beyond the sexuality, and beyond even the personality. What a powerful tool we have, and it is free. It doesn't cost us anything but the time to stop and spend a moment with ourselves and our creator.

I also paint a lot, which gets me to a meditative state as well. Once when I was painting, I had a vision that I was God, and the painting was me.

God asked me, the painting, "What is it you would like to be? I can make you a bird, I can make you a tree, or I can make you the woman sitting under the tree."

My response was, "Make me the woman sitting under the tree. Give me wings like the bird and strength like the tree."

God replied, "If you knew what it meant to be a woman, you wouldn't ask me for wings nor for strength, for a woman already bears great strength and already has the potential to fly."

I no longer pray with requests; instead, I spend time with God with the confidence in knowing that the more time I spend with him, the more I will know and accept myself and the creation that I am.

CHAPTER 12

The Search for Love

"I love you because the universe conspired to bring us together," he said.

"In your absence, I kiss the breeze in the hope that that breeze will find its way to your face, and you would feel the love from where it came, and you would feel my love," she replied.

I LOVE THESE lines from the book *The Alchemist*. You can feel the love in those words. I've always been a little old school when it comes to love. I often feel ahead of the times, but when it comes to love, I am an old-fashioned romantic. I want that shy, unhurried magic. I want passion. I want electricity.

One of the greatest miracles in life is love. I know it; you know it. We all know it. We all want it, we all desire it, and we all go a little crazy when we are in it or can't get it right. I don't think we really understand what love is, and that's what relationships are for. My grandmother once said to me, "No one will love you properly unless they love God too because God is love, and the only way to get closer to love is to get closer to God." She would often recite 1 Corinthians 13:4–8:

> Love is patient and kind; love does not envy or boast;
> it is not arrogant or rude. It does not insist on its own
> way; it is not irritable or resentful; it does not rejoice
> at wrongdoing, but rejoices with the truth. Love bears
> all things, believes all things, hopes all things, endures
> all things. Love never ends.

I've never forgotten what she said to me, each word spoken with the unwavering trust of one who knows completely. My relationships have shown me that when people don't believe in anything beyond themselves, they don't really understand love and will never really believe in you. Our ideas and beliefs are the driving force of our very existence.

I have considered myself unlucky in romantic love for a lot of my life. I wasn't able to be who I was, and so my first relationships were disguises, while my first true loves were hidden in my heart, their impossibility a constant throb of despair. I was dating a boy while my heart belonged to her. He would kiss me, and I would close my eyes and think of her, and he would know I was elsewhere. My boyfriends were never with me for very long; it was because I couldn't fake the chemistry. It's no surprise really, and I am sorry to myself and to them for behaving this way. For years, I gave up on love; during my years of "gay rehabilitation," I chose to be single, as it wouldn't be fair on either of us. Through all the turmoil and confusion, I would often pacify myself with the hope that one day, I could be with someone I loved and who loved me, and it would be real love, like the kind my grandmother told me about.

I am really lucky for someone so unlucky in love. I have seen such wonderful examples of love in my family. Both my grandparents were really in love. After they married, my mum was born, and then my grandfather was sent to war for a very long time. She would tell me how lonely she got sometimes and that she prayed every day that he wasn't hurt or cold or lonely. Sometimes, she prayed for him twice a day because she longed for him so much. War showed my grandparents how fleeting and fragile life is and that love is all that's worth holding onto.

At the end of their life, they would imagine leaving the earth together, hoping to be spared the heartache of loss. They had already lost two children and didn't want to have to bury their other half. My grandfather passed before my grandmother; he was ninety-four, and then Nonna joined him shortly after, at ninety-seven.

My parents are still very much in love; my father absolutely adores my mother. I feel blessed to have been moved by love in my family, despite being unlucky in love myself. Once I truly accepted myself, deciding that my sexuality was here to stay, I was inspired to find the one. Clearly, there were still unresolved issues within myself, as I repeatedly attracted repressed women who were confused, married, in the closet, or all three. In many respects, I felt like I was learning about love and began to perceive a clearer vision of what I did and didn't want, what I would and would not accept. Life is funny like that. Life is complicated sometimes, and so are women. I had to ask myself what I wanted in a partner, and the truth is that we must first learn to love ourselves.

For years, I tried loving myself but didn't know how. I didn't even like myself. I could blame everyone else in my life for feeling this way, as I spent a lot of my early years feeling unacceptable to others in many respects, but self-love continued to elude me until I took responsibility. I am responsible for loving myself, and I am responsible for the choices I made regarding how I feel about myself. I have learnt a lot about self-love: what it is, where it comes from, and how it must be maintained in order to live a satisfying life. I first had to discover how I really felt about love and my beliefs surrounding love.

In doing this, I discovered that my ideas about love were very conditional and very performance based. I also associate love with a magical feeling, an unexplainable high. I must say I did feel a high in my near-death experience. The experience involved shedding things that really didn't matter, like jealousy, sadness, pain, and bad memories. Energetically, I was in the presence of what felt like unconditional, overpowering (in a good way), and divine love. I was in a state of peace and harmony with life, and it brought on a profound sense of euphoria.

This kind of love is self-saturating. It flows from source to you and back again. This kind of love multiplies and expands when shared and need not be controlled, bargained with, or exploited. This kind of love is real love. All the other moments of perceived love are just pieces of love, broken by limitations and expectations. Through our relationships, these shards of love reveal a little more through every lesson, piece by piece, until we know that love is whole. These lessons are not subject to time and could be learnt in an instant of revelation, for divine love lives in the eternal present.

I discovered that this state can exist here on earth, if we have the courage to detach from the stumbling blocks that we perceive to be more important, like desire, anger, sadness, and insecurity. Basically, anything that makes you feel bad is an alarm bell, asking you to let go of whatever it is making you feel this way and transmute it into love. Everything we feel is our choice. Make the choice for joy. Choose peace. No matter what is going on in the outside world, nothing can take away our choice for peace. This is truly what we all desire; we just have trouble separating from the negativity in our lives. In fact, most of the time, we enjoy the contrast and revel in the dizzying pendulum of duality.

During my awakening (referred to in chapter 1), I arrived at work just as the sun was emerging over the horizon; all was silent. My job did not feel like it was my own. It felt like someone else's life. I asked the universe, God, if I am meant to be on another path and to give me a sign, to reveal the way. I thought of the two things I love doing most: designing and painting. As early as I can remember, I always drew, wrote poetry and stories, and paint using different materials. I was highly creative and expressed it in many ways.

That didn't change as I got older; in fact, after high school, I studied design at college. It was a selective school and difficult to get in. I remember being so nervous for my interview. The dean was somewhat of a celebrity, and I couldn't believe I was up next to be alone in a room with her. After my name was called, I walked timidly across the striking timber flooring, took a very deep breath, closed my eyes in prayer, and went in to her office.

"*Ciao,* Skyara," she called energetically as I entered the room.

I smiled and said hello and apologised for being nervous. She was welcoming and made me feel at home. She asked me several personal questions about what part of Italy I was from and about my family and upbringing. I relaxed after a bit of conversation, and then she asked what I had to show her. I gave her my design and technology assignment from year twelve, and she flicked through it with disinterest.

Then she asked, "What's that?" pointing to the sketch pad on my lap. "That's what I want to see."

It was a last-minute thought to bring my sketch pad along, but I thought I could show her what goes on in my head. As she went from page to page, a lot slower this time, she said words like "Interesting" and "Oh, wow." I was thrilled she seemed to like my sketches.

She looked up at me, removed her glasses, paused for a few seconds, and said, "You're going to be the Donatella Versace of Australia. You're in; I'll let the girls know."

I was exhilarated and couldn't wait to start design school. I completed three wonderful years in design school, but getting a job in fashion was hard, and so I ended up working as a chef and became fully qualified in that too. I had always dabbled in restaurants, as several of my cousins owned them, and I had experience in the field. They were my first jobs and paid well. I figured this would be a money maker until I could get into fashion and art.

Life crept on, and I kept working, and my dream kept dying, until the flame was kindled again on this particular morning, the morning after my awakening. I felt excitement in the possibility of "what if," followed by an inspired moment of faith that it actually could happen. Two weeks passed, and I got an opportunity to participate in a fashion show in Sydney. I could debut my collection in front of an audience with the potential of being recognised as a designer. I felt like the universe had offered me a rare window of opportunity, and so I decided to give it a shot. It was hard work, as I was already running a business and now had to design and produce a collection outside work hours.

Around a month later, a couple came into my café and offered to buy it; my partners and I ended up accepting their offer. The date of the settlement just so happened to be the day of the fashion show. *Were the signs always this obvious?* I thought to myself. I worked full time, day and night, in preparation for the show, and it was tiring. There were several nights I was unable to sleep, despite my exhaustion. The day was fast approaching, and I had to get ready for it emotionally and mentally. I ate healthy and trained a lot. When the day arrived, I wasn't sure how I truly felt, as I was so overtired and looked forward for my long-awaited moment to actually be over.

Once I got set up for my part of the show, I noticed that the first three rows of chairs were full of celebrities. Some of the models wearing my clothes were celebrities too. My eyes widened, and I became incredibly nervous. I chose to focus on the show instead and just do what I had come to do. I was the underdog in the show: the designer no one had heard of, someone who didn't even have a social media presence.

The night was amazing; I was eighth on the list to come out and present. When my collection came out, the crowd showed their appreciation, and the moment was epic. At the end of the show, I got the opportunity to dress some celebrities, and it was all very surreal. I felt like all my dreams had come true. I was on my way. About a month after the show, orders started coming in for clothing (not many, but enough to keep me going). About three months after the show, I received a call from the show coordinator, congratulating me for my success at the Sydney show and asking me if I wanted to do the New York show. I accepted and felt as though I was really on my way.

My collection was received incredibly well in New York, but what should have been a beautiful experience was overshadowed by three terrible agents. The first backed out of the show, the second took all her fees in advance only to run away with the money (without fulfilling any of her contractual obligations), and the third agent (a friend of over twenty years) accompanied me to New York but made the trip unbearable with behaviour that seemed to come from a place of jealousy.

My cousins also accompanied me; they were my saving grace, supporting me throughout the ordeal. I couldn't understand how I created these circumstances, but after further reflection, I saw it all as a combination of two contributing factors. The first factor is that the negative people who sabotaged my trip to New York were maybe a reflection of my own insecurities about this new career path. Maybe I secretly wanted it sabotaged. The second factor is my own innocence and naivety; I failed to recognise the opportunists in this cutthroat industry.

When I arrived in Sydney after the New York show, I gazed up at the sky, and it looked a lot like the time I had been at the café and asked for my dream to come true, only this time, everything inside me was different. My heart was no longer buzzing with inspiration and excitement; it was now wallowing in the disappointment of all my unanswered questions.

I went home from the airport and cried for a solid week. I didn't want to get out of bed. I decided I was going to give it up and go back to work. My heart was breaking whilst deciding this, but I didn't know what else to do. I had always worked well as a chef; occasionally, I would visit people at different nursing homes. Some I knew, and some I didn't. I don't know why I did this, but it seemed to make me feel better, and they had such wisdom to pass on. A friend of mine had mentioned that an aged care facility was trying to fill a chef position, and so I decided to give that a go.

This role would serve as my next learning ground; countless times, I deepened my understanding of love. There are many levels of love, and the level I experienced in this aged care home was one of the highest. I served the residents as best I could, and they always enjoyed my cooking (most of them, anyway. Some would wake up like Angry Anderson; there was no way to make them happy, and that's just how it was.).

There were some, however, who made it evident that you were all they had in this world. Their families had abandoned them, or they didn't have any family, but somehow, they made you feel like all they had left in this world was you. They had reached an age where they had truly lived their lives and spent a lot of time in reflection. For many of them, their lives were full and their hearts even fuller, and they had no one else to share it with except you. There were so many awe-inspiring moments at work. I was showered with so much love that I would get choked up from time to time.

One time, I made chocolate chip muffins and kept four without chocolate to give to a woman who was allergic to chocolate. She was so moved by my gesture that she went out and bought me a present. I told her I was just doing my job, but she insisted I take the gift, and she pulled my head in and kissed my forehead while sharing how she felt about me about me and how special I was to her. When she hugged me, I could feel the love she was sending me; it washed over my entire being like the warmth of the sun. I was so moved.

Many of my elderly friends have helped shape my faith in the idea that we all return to love. They still have all this love to give; in fact, they have so much more love to give because at the end of it all, they realise that love is the reason we are here. This is why we exist; it becomes so much clearer when we are nearing the end of our lives.

This place filled with forgotten souls taught me a great deal about love.

Our ideas on love are ever changing and evolving. The more illusions we shed about ourselves and others, the deeper and purer our ideas of love become. How incredible must love truly be if we are so overwhelmed by its lower expressions. The more I learn about love, the more I realise how little I know. I am forever learning more. I am learning to change my perspective, understand my needs, and forgive my own mistakes when it comes to love.

There are certain things about myself I know for sure. One-night stands are not for me. Personally, this expression of love is far too superficial. I love everyone, just differing degrees; I love to be around some people more than others, but I do actually love everyone, even those who have challenged me. I love deeply and intensely; that's just me. I am gullible and choose to believe in everyone, including myself, even those who fail to believe in themselves. I have learnt to listen to my own intuition when it comes to love. Romantic love is blind, and it's especially blind to the opinions of others. If only we could have that kind of wilfulness when it comes to our dreams. Someone tells you not to date someone because they're bad news, and it makes you want them all the more. Someone tells you that you're unable to do something, and you stop, listen, and even believe it yourself. If only we could blind ourselves to the opinions, expectations, and judgements of others and follow our hearts.

We learn about love, not only through relationships, but also through what we love to do. The Bible says that where your treasure is, there your heart is also. I have come to believe this completely. For so many years, I ignored my heart. I would have a crush on someone and would want to act on my feelings or say something, but I just couldn't because for so long, I believed I was ill with homosexuality. I ignored my natural impulses and hoped the feelings would go away. The freedom I have now is daunting because when my heart beats for someone and I'm not sure why, whether it be a crush or friendship, something inside me still holds back. I have to learn to let go of that.

I am getting better at telling people I love them, even if they are just friends. I am better at sharing my feelings and telling someone how I feel. I am also better at overlooking the projections and judgements of others. If my heart is pulling me towards someone and my friends suggest it's a bad idea, I need to trust my heart, no matter what. Come what may, I will not forgive myself for ignoring my heart again. If I suffer rejection as a consequence, then it was meant to be, and I was meant to go through that. I feel freer living this way, but making a move or expressing what is in your heart is never easy. As soon as the information leaves your heart and exits your mouth, you become vulnerable and open. I have come to see this as a beautiful strength and not a debilitating weakness.

Many of my sentiments on love could be summarised by *Golden*, a movie made recently about a golden boy. The boy was born gold, different from his siblings. He was special. As he grew up, he realised that others were not like him; he was unique. Life went on, and he found it hard being golden, so unlike everyone else. Things became more difficult, and he decided to focus on other things like his education. He moved to a university far away from where he grew up. One day, as he was walking through the new city, he caught the eye of another man. The two men looked at each other intensely, realising that they were both made of gold. They were different but the same. It was as though they found a home within each other; they belonged.

For me, love is like this. It's a simple message, but it is so true. We are all longing for acceptance and love. The irony is that this acceptance and love is only found when we learn to love and accept others.

I don't want someone exactly like me; in fact, I asked for that once, and the most interesting thing occurred (be careful what you wish for). I soon met this woman who I felt an instant connection with (I have come to realise it wasn't so much a connection as it was familiarity). She was so like me in so many ways; we even shared the same birthday. After knowing her a short while, I realised I didn't like many of her qualities; these dislikes were a reflection of what I didn't like within myself. We enjoyed many of the same things, we had similar creative talents, and we would often speak at the same time (which became increasingly annoying). We also both had issues that we dealt with very differently, which was an eye-opener, as well. We both had a very similar level of emotional weight and were both inclined to fill the void destructively, though through different means (she had addictions of the chemical kind and I had addictions of the food kind).

This relationship was a mirror for me; it taught me a great deal about myself. Every relationship and every personality has something very important to teach us about ourselves. Each and every one of our relationships, whether acquaintance, close friend, family, or even complete stranger, should never be undervalued. Each comes with very different lessons.

In *The Alchemist*, Santiago goes to a well and meets a girl fetching water; he knew instantly he was in love and told her. He said, "I love you," before ever getting to know her. I had never thought about this concept before reading *The Alchemist*, but I do believe you always know when you truly love someone, even before knowing the person. Love at first sight could be closer to seeing the real truth about each other, more so than after twenty years in a relationship. What do we find out in those twenty years? Our likes, dislikes, behaviours, vices, ideas, beliefs, and perspectives are not who are. I feel we see the essence of what we are in these love-at-first-sight moments.

By telling the girl, "I love you because the universe conspired to bring us together," he opened himself up to her. Being in love teaches us how to open up to love. Divine love has always been deep, but our ability to understand it has been stifled by our distorted ideas. It seems we still need to experience rejection to know that love does not need to be secured and controlled. It seems we need to experience the superficial expressions of love, like sexuality, before we can transform these primal desires into an intimacy with all living things. Love needs to be free and expressed, and when it is, it is scary but also liberating.

Loving like this sets you free from all fears, including rejection. There have been times when I have loved someone, only to have them not reciprocate. Did it hurt? Of course. Was I free and at peace with myself? Yes, very much so. I have also been in the position where someone loved me, but I didn't love them in the same way. I found myself wanting to comfort them because I saw how much they wanted my love. In these circumstances, I have learnt that honestly is the best policy. I was completely honest with my feelings towards them.

I told one woman in particular that my love for her was not the same as hers was for me. I wished her all the happiness of finding someone who would love her in the same way. She argued the point and suggested that love might grow; I listened to her and stayed, but when it didn't grow, I felt worse leaving her later on.

It seems like love is never balanced, but it is our ideas about love that are unbalanced. We must stop mistaking romantic love for divine love. Romantic love can definitely teach us about divine love, but ultimately, romantic love is tainted with our desperation, our insecurities, our longing for acceptance: essentially, our need for divine love. In our search for divine love, we cannot overlook romantic love, but the problem in our society today is that we place all importance on romantic love, as though it is the pinnacle of human endeavour.

Even our art, literature, and music reflect this enormous emphasis on romantic love. Once we find what we are looking for in a partner, we often destroy the relationship by methodically putting all our longings onto the shoulders of our partner: a tremendous amount of responsibility. What was once in human history the responsibility of an entire village or community now rests on just one person. In our partner, we expect to secure love, a sense of belonging, a sense of purpose, sexual gratification, emotional support, a best friend, a mentor: The list goes on. We must learn how to surrender to divine love so that our romantic relationships become about growth and freedom rather than comfort and attachment.

I love very deeply, so the loneliness only grew, and my heart would hurt, knowing that I had turned love into something cheap. As I got older, when everyone around me was in a panic about marriage and children and their biological clock ticking, I decided to stay single. I chose to be on my own and feel the feelings that came. I tried to focus on my work, my family, and my dreams. I tried to get to know myself better and evaluate myself and reflect on everything I had learnt thus far.

The truth is that there were many moments of loneliness; many moments of sitting down to watch a movie and wishing I had someone in my arms or being in theirs, telling someone I love them, and coming home to cook for them. It was hard at times, and there were tears that came and went, but I began to see that this sadness was coming from a perceived lack within myself. I started to cook for myself, spent time in reflection getting to know myself better, and overall, cultivated a sense of wholeness, learning how to love myself. We need to feel as whole as possible before a romantic relationship; otherwise, we just end up seeking what is missing within. It's interesting because when you feel whole, there is clarity. When a person enters your world, you can feel whether they're the one to join with or not. You get a better sense of other energies entering your domain; then you get a feel of whether you can grow together and whether your romantic love will teach divine love or extend the void of longing.

I wanted to end this chapter with one of my favourite love poems: *Annabelle Lee*. My favourite part of this poem is a verse I find so powerful:

But our love it was stronger by far than the love
Of those who were older than we—
Of many far wiser than we—
And neither the angels in Heaven above,
Nor the demons down under the sea,
Can ever dissever my soul from the soul

Of the beautiful Annabel Lee.

In this poem, Edgar Allan Poe speaks about how powerful love is; he believed in this love so much that death didn't stop his love; in fact, he slept near her tomb, showing how strong his love was. Love can be a rough ride; it has its peaks and valleys, but when it is real love, it truly is forever and not just in this physical life, but even in eternity. I believe that love is so strong that it transcends time and space; in each life we take on, we search for the love of those we felt it with first since the beginning of time. Our heart yearns for them in each lifetime and seeks to find them in whatever body they present themselves. "Honour," "respect," and "awe" are words associated with this kind of love.

I choose to believe in this kind of love. I know my one will find me, and I will find her, and our love will transcend all time and space when we realise that in each other, we are home.

Annabel Lee
By Edgar Allan Poe
It was many and many a year ago,
In a kingdom by the sea,
That a maiden there lived whom you may know
By the name of ANNABEL LEE; —
And this maiden she lived with no other thought
Than to love and be loved by me.

Skyara Reign

She was a child and I was a child,
In this kingdom by the sea,
But we loved with a love that was more than love—
I and my Annabel Lee—
With a love that the winged seraphs of heaven
Coveted her and me.

And this was the reason that, long ago,
In this kingdom by the sea,
A wind blew out of a cloud by night
Chilling my Annabel Lee;
So that her high-born kinsman came
And bore her away from me,
To shut her up in a sepulchre
In this kingdom by the sea.

The angels, not half so happy in Heaven,
Went envying her and me: —
Yes! — that was the reason (as all men know,
In this kingdom by the sea)
That the wind came out of a cloud by night,
chilling and killing my Annabel Lee.

But our love it was stronger by far than the love
Of those who were older than we—
Of many far wiser than we—
And neither the angels in Heaven above,
Nor the demons down under the sea,
Can ever dissever my soul from the soul
Of the beautiful Annabel Lee: —

For the moon never beams without bringing me dreams
Of the beautiful Annabel Lee;
And the stars never rise but I see the bright eyes
Of the beautiful Annabel Lee;
And so, all the night-tide, I lie down by the side
Of my darling, — my darling — my life and my bride,
In her sepulchre there by the sea—
In her tomb by the side of the sea.

CHAPTER 13

Unconditional Love

WHY DO WE go through life, experiencing distortions of love? "Distortion" is the action of giving a misleading account or impression. When love is real, the experience is felt and known on every level of your being: spiritual, physical, emotional, and mental. You know love when it "feels" right. For me, this subject is so simple and yet so complicated. Do we love each other *through* our own distortions, and if so, how do we love from our essence, our purest form? I have learnt that unconditional love can only really come from one place, and that is spirit. Spirit coexists with unconditional love in its purest form; call it God or the universe. The Holy Spirit is the voice for God. It speaks for heaven, which is our highest reality, but also understands our illusions without believing in them (i.e., the world of form, of matter). It is this voice that always brings peace. It is this voice that comforts us in those moments when we know that everything is perfect, that somehow we are completely looked after and divinely guided towards our highest good, if only we could let go of the need to control and surrender to his voice. We must learn to choose spirit's voice over the voice of the ego. The voice of the ego seeks to attack, blame, control, and limit. Is this what we truly want from our relationships?

There is a threefold purpose for sex, outlined in most resources about sacred sex. The first is "generation," meaning procreation; the second is "regeneration," meaning for good health; and the third and most important is "spiritualisation," meaning the elevation of consciousness and ultimate transcendence of sexuality through tantric principles. Articles on sacred sexuality often miss the point and still focus on the lower, base chakra vibration of sexuality. The point is to move the energy up through the higher chakras, similar to kundalini meditation, with the intention of experiencing higher vibrations of love that transcend lust, power, control, security, and survival.

We forget that sex is a sacrament.

Through my studies on sacred sexuality, the intention and purpose related to sex is transcending the physical and experiencing the bliss and enlightenment of our eternal selves. Sex is a gift we can give to each other as souls. Sex itself could be an experience of absolute peace and perfect love, but we have reduced it to a strictly physical act, being touched a certain way, reaching orgasm at a certain time, essentially using sex only for physical pleasure. How much have we diminished love through sex with our modern-day distortions?

It is my belief that this has happened because we fail to see ourselves through the eyes of God. Through our souls, the place where God resides, we can begin to "see" each other as the embodiment of unconditional love. Through sacred sex, we can reach a higher understanding of love, experiencing the bliss of unity without the dark distortions and disempowering taboos that society has placed around sex.

A friend of mine recently said that she fails to hear the voice of God when it comes to sex and relationships, but she hears it clearly in every other aspect of her life. I found this idea fascinating and found myself exploring it for days. I couldn't get it off my mind. My immediate response was, "Maybe God is wanting to put you in a relationship where you will hear his voice."

I spent days evaluating my own response. I believe God speaks to us all the time, every moment of every day. I also believe that we tune in and we tune out voluntarily. Like everything else in life, sometimes when we stray from our most desired path, whether we know it or not, it's because we stopped listening and allowed for something else to take the lead in our lives. There are many replacements for the voice of God in our world, but none of them could ever measure up. We often need to find this out the hard way, for ourselves, before we understand that the voice of God is our highest good, our highest desire, our greatest success, and always our highest intention. When we fight God, we are really fighting ourselves from being on the path of perfection and pure intent.

Our belief systems have a lot to do with how the ideas of love become distorted. I have two personal examples. I grew up a Catholic, surrounded by devout Catholic friends and family. A close friend of the family had groomed one of their sons to become a priest. I grew up knowing this boy and also spent some time with him as a man, and I often thought to myself that he was a good-looking, nice, and respectful guy; why should he be deprived of experiencing life in all its fullness? I couldn't understand why priests weren't allowed to marry and have children. I often wondered how this was an example of love. If God is love, we need to learn more about it. How can we learn about love without loving relationships?

I watched him grow into a man and witnessed how deprivation affects our mental, physical, and spiritual states. When he counselled me on my sexuality, I remember clearly the conversation making no sense. I had been made to go and have confession with him downstairs in my mothers' house; he was trying to put me on the straight and narrow, and yet I could feel and see his own suffering. His advice to me was to stay celibate if I had "those desires" or to try and make it work with a man, and if all else fails, become a nun. Funnily enough, I considered being a nun briefly, thinking that it may remove me from my family for a while and allow me the freedom to really discover who I was.

Whatever his personal issues were, it felt like he was giving me the only advice he personally knew, or this is possibly how he dealt with things, by becoming a priest. I remember him speaking to me about sexuality and in particular, his interpretation of biblical beliefs on the subject, as well as his own. He spoke about it in a very condemning way, in the sense that he compared sexuality to our dark side, an illness of our time, and also made it sound like a very perverted subject. He spoke about it in almost disgust. There definitely is a darker side to sex, just like everything else in this dualistic world, but as with everything else, it's all about intention.

I intend to know God through everything, including sex. We only truly learn through experience. We can never learn through the distorted ideas and interpretations of others. This instance reminded me of a question I had asked my father. I asked him why he stopped reading the Bible after only picking it up for a brief moment. He honestly responded that he found it too hard to understand; he was obviously not equipped to handle such reading, and so like all other Catholics, he entrusted the teachings of this hard scripture to the priests who preached on it.

In *A New Earth*, Eckhardt Tolle said that as soon as you add words and explanations to understanding God, everything loses its meaning. I believe this to be true.

I personally enjoy reading the Bible; through my life experiences, I have come to know more deeply what was intended by the stories and who God really is. I also understand that to read any Holy Scripture, it is so important to pray and ask God to show you who he truly is and to ask the Holy Spirit to guide your thoughts as you read.

My priest friend had his own interpretation of sexuality; I believe that one of the reasons for this distortion was in his own personal suffering with deprivation. I believe that many other distortions within the Catholic church are a direct result of the denial of natural human conditions such as celibacy, remembering that one of the benefits of sex is for well-being, mental health in particular. In articulating this, my goal is not to shame or hurt anyone, in particular the Catholic church I grew up in. It is to share my truth from my perspective, in the hope that it will end some suffering for people who have limiting and guilt-laden beliefs.

My second personal experience with this is my own deprivation of love and sexuality. I had a night out with some old friends some time ago; one of them was a crush of mine when I was in my late teens. I met her at the gym, and all I could think about was how beautiful she was and how I wanted to spend time with her and get to know her better. We became friends, and she opened me up to a new world, a world of absolute freedom (worldly freedom). She was so comfortable with herself, and from the conservative, strict Italian, and Catholic household I grew up in, she was crazy, and I loved it. She showed me a world where there were no limits; it was all about living in the moment and experiencing everything that we are naturally drawn to. I needed this in my life, and it assisted me in letting go of the guilt I carried associated with

Eventually, I would be released from the bondage of past conditioning and was able to explore natural longings without guilt or fear. At the time, though, I was afraid, and so I shut down any crush I had and made sure any desires never came out.

In my later years, I caught up with her and our old friends, and although it felt like no time had passed, I had changed dramatically, and I saw it in this moment. She pointed out that one of the reasons I may be struggling to settle down and find love was because I was now living and experiencing my younger years as an adult. Events such as meeting someone, having your first sexual experience, sharing in a kiss, experimenting with sexuality, experimenting with life, and so on, had all been put on hold while I concentrated on work instead. In my late twenties and early thirties, I was catching up on what would normally happen after puberty. I numbed this aspect of myself.

This reminded me of an older woman I met who had come out at fifty years old. Her reaction to understanding she was gay was to quickly marry the first girl who came along. After the wedding, she soon understood that her partner was just her first kiss, and it was the beginning of her exploration. It was too late, though; they were married, and she felt morally obliged to stay committed.

I remember seeing this unfold; I watched her flirt with other women and play these games that I recognised from my friends in their teens. When you're fifteen or sixteen years old, you don't marry the first person you meet. What I was witnessing was the effects of deprivation because of false beliefs, really the beliefs that we could never be ourselves. I feel this is what happened to me, and I suppose I'm thankful it happened in my twenties.

There came a point on my journey when my heart couldn't take it anymore. With the help of God, my heart broke free from its self-imposed prison and took over as my guide in life, helping me see my own uniqueness and brilliance; eventually, my walls and my strongholds crumbled to the ground. I was not able to explore meaningful romantic relationships until much later than normal, and as a result, my growth and development was delayed. I was now trying to catch up.

After having the courage to live from my heart, I experienced a lot and all at once, such as attraction, flirting, relationship dynamics, sexual experiences, understanding friendships, and so on. I am now finally doing all of this through an honest space: my authentic self. The adult in me wants to behave and settle down and find love, but my deprived, guilt-laden teenage self wants to come out and play and be free. Freedom isn't ever that far away, and it isn't terribly hard to find; it truly is the art of allowing yourself to just be, as you are. That is true freedom. I know this now. Youth rush through life whilst the elderly try and slow it down. This is a powerful lesson I learned from elderly people. It is never too late to stop, allow, and just be.

My past conditioning has inevitably led to other distortions of love, as well. My distortions came in the form of believing no one could love me because I was damaged goods; I had to now work hard to be seen and loved. Another distortion for me was in believing that pain had to come with love, and so I was always untrusting and paranoid when someone genuinely liked me and wanted to get to know me. I always assumed there was a motive behind their love.

Another distortion, and one I know many people suffer from, is this belief that we are never enough. Our society is very outcome based, and so surrender makes no sense to people. Most people use relationships to fill a void. We seek pleasure and pain in our relationships; many times, we seek the numbing comfort of disconnected companionship. Some of us seek drama in a relationship, and some of us seek partners we can mould to our own ideas of who they should be.

The most prevalent idea in the modern-day relationship is that our partner will comfort all feelings of scarcity and lack of love. Only God can do this. We have very unrealistic ideas when it comes to what we depend on our partners for. What used to be the role of an entire village (in our not-too-distant history) now rests on the shoulders of one person. Our partners are expected to provide us pleasure, comfort, feeling of belonging, sense of purpose, friendship, security, support, and guidance, just to name a few. What a heavy burden of expectation, in contrast to surrendering to love.

I have often caught myself unable to surrender my expectations; who doesn't want to know or have a guarantee that everything will work out? I have very much learnt that in life and love, surrender is where we all have to live if we want peace. Surrender is a fundamental foundation of unconditional love. Surrender forces you to just let it be.

I wanted to spend time in this chapter talking about sacred love and the kind we all yearn for in our soul. We all are sexual beings; we were created this way, and it is an essential part of our existence. Today, we have a profound difficulty associating sexuality with anything sacred; it's no wonder, considering the sexually driven world we live in. Seduction and enticement re tools used to make people do things they don't really want to do and need things they don't really need.

In lifetimes past, sex was used as a tool or vehicle for worship; in essence, the act of lovemaking could bring two people closer to God and closer to bliss. I find it interesting that the taboos of sex are what many people find most enticing about it. Where does this idea of dirty or forbidden come from in the first place? It's all about intention. Do you want to make love, or do you want to fuck? Excuse the vulgar expression, but I do find it a fitting way to describe a couple of bodies desperate to squeeze some fleeting, momentary pleasure from each other, without love.

From my own experience, sexual, spiritual, and creative energy are one. All three for me are states of bliss that bring me closer to God. Our expressions of spirit, sex, and creativity all can be enlightening moments in our lives, if driven by pure intention, but they can equally be destructive if lived out through our distorted beliefs. Sex is the most coveted experience in our existence. As humans, we yearn for it so badly that in our modern-day world, we pay for it, cheapen it, talk about it, watch it on all forms of media, dream about it, think up different ways to experience it, buy things because of it, and so on. It is so sought-after that it is addictive, and in the nature that most of us seek it, the pit is never ending, and our hunger only grows.

Why is it that after sex, people (especially men) still feel empty and almost immediately begin yearning again? I once felt this yearning even during a sexual experience; it was this experience that made me question what it was I was *really* yearning for. While my ex-girlfriend was cheating on me, when we would have sex, I felt like I wasn't enough. How could I be enough if she had to seek romantic love from other women as well? And although I loved her, she wasn't enough for me, either. My "not enough," however, was spiritual. I lost the connection to her. The bond that tied us together was broken for me. Her love was no longer mine, and my love was not enough for the both of us to make up the difference.

This experience revealed a seemingly obvious purpose for sexual union. Sex is empty without love. In this experience with my ex,

I also discovered that when love is no longer part of the equation, we become numb and unconscious, and so sex becomes a physical act; in reality, it's a watering-down of our divinity. Like many other instances when we choose to become unconscious, especially in our relationship, it's usually because our beliefs become distorted; we no longer see the divine being we love unconditionally, and we lose the connection that bound us together by failing to see each other.

When we become unconscious in our relationship, we no longer feel with our heart or our intuition, which are both connected to the divine; instead, we think with our mind, which is directly connected to ego and has been conditioned by this world. Our mind teaches us about pain and lack of love, while our heart and intuition show us our divinity in all its glory. I understand now that an imbalance of this vibration (or frequency) is what causes a relationship to disintegrate. Nothing is ever a mistake, though; only a lesson learnt.

The Bible talks about two people being evenly yoked, and I believe that this is exactly what that statement is trying to explain. 2 Corinthians 6:14 says not to be unevenly yoked because light cannot have a relationship with the darkness. Darkness is the absence of light. Where there is light, darkness cannot abide. I love this. What an example of the true meaning of balance. We seem to be engaged in a constant pull between light and dark, though in reality, we are always moving closer to God as we shed the layers of illusion (darkness) and allow more light in.

A healthy relationship should be based on this notion of shedding illusions and allowing more light in, constantly supporting each other's growth through unconditional love. My sister once taught me an important lesson on the value of things. I was going through a tough time with my break-up, in the sense that I was deciding whether to let go of the relationship. She asked me what the value of the seed I had planted was. I was confused at first, but then she elaborated and said that each time we begin something, we plant a seed. That seed is then nurtured by us and hopefully develops to its full potential. She then said that if the seed planted didn't bear the fruit that I thought it would, it should be discarded. However, if the seed had grown to its full potential and bore all the fruit I had expected, then it was worth fighting for because it contained value. All the effort, nurturing, and growing that took place in my relationship contained its value.

The truth is that sometimes people grow apart; some are only in your life to share some lessons, and that's perfectly okay too. This relationship taught me to let go when I needed to, when the seed that had grown was no longer producing fruit. The spirit of love is joy, peace, patience, kindness, goodness, and faithfulness; when the spirit of love is lost, the relationship is not worth keeping because love is no longer being expressed in its fullness. It is a cycle. If we are not at one with ourselves, we cannot be at one with another, and when we lose the connection to ourselves, we lose the connection to God, along with the ability to connect with others.

Love in its purest form is all-inclusive. We have grown into a society that values the material world over our internal world, but our internal world is where everything exists: our perceptions, feelings, beliefs, and ideas. If we own more, earn more, drive a nice car, or look a certain way, we think we are growing. The real value of a life is how much love it expressed, not how many things it accumulated. Spiritual teachers from all paths have demonstrated this truth. Working with the elderly has driven the point further for me. What truly matters in the end, when all turns to dust? Our spirits being eternal and the fact that the humble will be exalted and the boastful will be humbled. The meek shall inherit the earth. We are all here to learn and collect data, and so no one's journey is perfect. I personally try to always understand that when challenging circumstances or challenging people arrive, it is a blessing from the Holy Spirit, pushing me to shed more layers of illusion and receive a higher revelation of love.

Jesus told us to be the example, and even on his journey, didn't walk around criticising people or trying to correct all of humanity. He demonstrated unconditional love, as we all should (if we could just get over ourselves and remember our self). Jesus was all about inclusion. In my NDE encounter with him, I had never felt more accepted, more loved, more included, more cherished. May we grow in God and learn to love each other like this. May we see each other for the light we are.

The Journey to Freedom

THE PATHS WE must take for our liberation are incredibly personal and specific to each individual; however, there are some general ideas that I feel would be helpful for all when navigating through this often chaotic and confusing world. I am no expert, and I am beginning to see that as long as I am confined to this body, there will always be illusions and distortions to shed, but these ideas and practices support that goal. The journey is often difficult, but I'm driven by an unwavering faith for the betterment of me.

Seeking Truth

With regard to seeking truth, I want every Christian to hear me loud and clearly, especially Christians struggling with sexuality: Although the church contains some truth, it is not the entire truth, and it is perfectly okay to seek it elsewhere. For example, in my studies of theology, the Bible frequently speaks about the importance of meditation, and yet very little is spent on the subject or the practice of it. Meditation has been my life source. I began with five minutes and progressed to hours, even getting up super early to do it because that's how much it has impacted me. I realised in my meditations why it is so important: It is a chance to spend time with the source, God, the universe, or your divine self. In this moment, the connection and inspiration that occurs is life changing. In discovering God, we discover ourselves; that's the best way to put it, and it is truly the guidance I am most grateful for from my guru in chapter 1. Without this practice, I wouldn't have discovered my truest self. I wouldn't have learnt to love myself unconditionally because I finally saw myself through the eyes of God. I don't think I would be here to share this story if I hadn't taken her advice and practiced meditation. I encourage all readers to explore meditation, take classes, read about it, and practice and experience it for yourself.

I feel it is also very important to test the power of positivity and gratitude for yourself. We are so incredibly powerful in how we create that even the medical world can no longer deny the mind's ability to manifest disease or healing. I read *Life Visioning*, an amazing book by Michael Bernard Beckwith. He told a story about a woman who healed herself from kidney disease simply by thanking God for her kidneys. He said it so simply: "When was the last time you thanked God for your kidneys?"

This concept got me wondering about my own life and challenges, weight being one of them. I began implementing the following prayer after my morning walks:

"God, thank you for my fast metabolism; thank you for my high-functioning digestive system. Thank you for my health, and thank you that I have the strength and motivation to get up and go for walks and train. Thank you for helping me understand how to look after the temple you have allowed me to enter, and thank you that you are teaching me daily how to work with it and not against it. I also thank you for the self-love I am learning, that this self-love helps me not seek comfort in unhealthy foods and unhealthy eating habits; instead, I find comfort within myself, really knowing that I already have all I need, and there is no need for excessiveness. Thank you that

I am blessed abundantly and that there is no need to overindulge, but where I have my weaknesses, you help my body compensate and work a little harder to satisfy the need. Thank you that tomorrow is a new day and I can forgive myself for messing up today. Thank you for helping me desire nutritious and wholesome food that blesses me and makes me feel amazing."

Each day, I would be grateful for the unending grace I experienced in meditation, grace I gave myself in the understanding that we are all simply on a journey and navigating the best we can. I found with my weight loss that a lot of my weight was somehow connected to the weight I carried for others as well as myself, weight that was mostly a mixture of burdens, guilt, and shame. I have learnt to release these, and in turn, my body released some weight too.

I also had to learn to love myself and where I was at; I found this the hardest to do. In doing so, I could in essence love myself to wholeness. I could love myself so much that I wouldn't need anyone or anything (namely food) to fill any need in me because the needs are met by me. Michael explains how to meditate and ask questions and receive inspiration directly from our intuition; this is called life visioning.

After trying it for several days and asking God what my highest purpose is for this life, I was given an answer which astonished me. God told me that I am here to teach unconditional self-love. We are not really taught this in our societies and families; self-love is the beginning of everything. I came out of that meditation very upset, with an incredibly loud "No!" reverberating in my skull. How could this be my life purpose when I don't even love myself? I don't even know how to love myself; how could I teach others?

I dwelt on this for days and then weeks and then months. In another meditation, I discovered that all my life lessons really were lessons on how to love myself again; funny, that. After all I had experienced, how did I manage to find it within myself to love me? The answer, like most, is so simple and yet so complicated.

Only through the eyes of God can we see ourselves with eyes of unconditional love. My journey of self-love is really about finding my divinity and understanding that I am divine and that I am a unique creation of God, who is the unexplainable, awe-inspiring energy source of unending and unconditional love. It is that love from which I was created, and from that place, I can see myself with love. I see me now and love me. I return to the physical and the nagging of my ego that tells me I'm not good enough and takes away my peace, but I can bring that divinity to earth, hold it in my heart, and know that this love is the only thing that gives life real meaning. We are here for too short a time to not live from this place of unconditional love. It is in this place where we truly understand that we are all one. We are all brothers and sisters. It is here we learn to love one another and love ourselves. I now know what Jesus meant when he said that we must treat others as we would want to be treated, but we can only do so if we love ourselves.

My encouragement is to seek the truth, however you may need to. Seek it, and seek it with all your heart because the truth leads to freedom. On my journey, I have visited counsellors, psychologists, spiritual teachers, meditation teachers, psychics, and clairvoyants. I have found truths with many of them. I have to warn anyone against seeking help through a religious organisation, as this was a very destructive path for me. I went to a Christian counsellor seeking help for my sexuality and abuse as a child, among other things; the sessions were horrible. As nice as she appeared to be, her words cut me deeply. It was as though, in the nicest way possible, she was trying to let me know how much of an abomination I was to God. Everything seemed to be my fault, including my abuse as a child. She repeatedly told me that I could change and that I was being stubborn in not wanting to give up homosexuality, as though it were cigarettes. I spent a month with her, twice a week, until I couldn't take it anymore and went to a non-Christian counsellor, who told me that homosexuality was not "changeable." I didn't feel much relief from her, either, because she had some homophobia issues and treated it as though I was doomed to deal with this circumstance. I had the most relief when I heard the truth at thirty-three years old from a spiritual teacher I met at a seminar. She was the first person to tell me that I am a blessing just as I am and that sexuality is a part of me, not all of me. She was the first person to show me who I am in the light of truth: a perfect creation of God.

CHAPTER 15

Living in Spirit

Defining Spirit

BEFORE WE BEGIN, let us not get lost in differing terminologies. Let me clarify that when I use the word "God," I mean divine love. When I use the word "spirit," I mean divine channel of communication or connection to divine love. There may be infinite paths that lead to our enlightenment. This earth has been blessed to receive countless holy scriptures and even more holy messengers who have discovered truth. Truth, however simple in essence, is multifaceted and incredibly difficult to reveal through the limitations of mind and matter, let alone language. Although our eternal self is the same in essence, our temporary self is completely unique and diverse with varying levels of physical, mental, and emotional predispositions, and our personal experience thus far will clearly play a decisive role in our perception, values, beliefs, and ideas. There is a path to happiness for every individual, and every individual draws on divine inspiration differently. Your connection to divine love may be through God, higher self, an owl, a lion, Buddha, Christ, a giant flying spaghetti monster (actually a divine being in the registered social movement of Pastafarianism), Krishna, Shiva, Holy Spirit, and so on. The terminology doesn't matter. Recognising the voice of divine love is what truly matters. Being able to identify the voice of the ego and choose otherwise is what's important. God is truly in everything.

It is also important to recognise that your temporary self is not a very good decision maker; you need to surrender your life to spirit. The twelve-step program is undoubtedly the most universally used and most successful program for reprogramming addictions; the entire program is founded on surrendering to a higher power. You often make the same mistakes over and over again; you suffer because of your expectations of others and what you think you want from life. Sometimes, you need to be taken to the depths of despair before surrendering to spirit. You surrender honestly and whole-heartedly, experiencing true peace despite your circumstances, but as soon as life gets comfortable again, you forget to live through spirit and start making decisions, forming expectations, and having desires from your fractured temporary self.

Spirit is outside of our temporary consciousness and yet is also a part of us and within us always. How is this possible? It is the same for our permanent self and eternal self. Imagine a small circle inside a larger circle. The smaller circle erepresents our temporary self, and the larger our eternal self. Our eternal self is always within us, and yet our self-imposed illusions prevent us from knowing the entirety of our eternal self. As we remove the illusions, we expand to contain more of our eternal self.

Living in Spirit

In this world of duality, our perceptions, values, beliefs, and ideas are directed by one of two voices: the voice of the ego or the voice of spirit. We must develop the awareness to perceive both voices and the willingness to choose only one voice. This is difficult to begin with, for spirit's voice is quiet. It speaks of peace. The ego's voice is loud because it is threatened. It is constantly threatened with annihilation because we made it and can easily unmake it. We are creatures of habit, and the habit of hearing the ego's voice is deeply engrained. Native American Indians told a story of the two wolves within us all; one is evil and the other is good. When their youth asked which wolf would prevail, the answer was simply, "Whichever one you feed."

We must create daily and moment-to-moment habits of self-observation and acceptance in order to feed our good wolf. Our minds cannot serve two masters. We are given these opportunities through every aspect of life, from how we perceive our internal world to how we perceive our external world. The voice of spirit speaks to us through everything, through the events in our life: our relationships, a movie we saw, a book we read, a goal we reached, a mistake we made, a kiss, a moment of rage, our successes and our failures, helping a brother or sister, the ocean, a breeze, a bird flying through the clouds, a sunrise, a sunset.

In each and every moment, we are deciding which voice should be our guide, the voice of the ego or the voice of spirit. In each moment, we are either learning who we truly are and shedding the layers of illusion or forgetting who we are and adding more layers to the illusion. Every interaction we have reveals which voice we serve. Through anger or judgement, we are serving the ego. Through love and compassion, we are serving spirit. To perceive which voice it is that guides us, we must develop awareness.

Awareness

One of the greatest barriers for awareness is reactivity. We hardly ever really act but are constantly reacting to stimulus, based on our past experiences and conditioning. We often know we should be taking a new path, and yet when the moment arrives, we react as we always have. If we have not started developing our awareness, we can only identify the reaction after it has occurred, if at all. Our greatest ally for preventing reactivity is being present because our reactions are based on the past. Developing the awareness of breath and sensation is one very effective way of being present.

We should also be constantly engaged in observing our thoughts and emotions. Most of the time, our mind is out of control and our emotions unchecked, so instead of acting with purpose and through spirit, we react through the ego. A reaction always begins physically with a sensation in the body; it becomes a thought, then an emotion, and finally a reaction. If we practice observing breath, sensation, thought, and emotion, we can be in constant awareness of the entire process. With practice, we are able to stop ourselves from externalising the reaction.

We have now prevented harming others, but we are still harming ourselves if we cannot accept internal sensations, thoughts, and emotions. Once we can remove ourselves from the sensations, thoughts, and emotions, we can observe them objectively without identifying ourselves within them. They are not who we are, and they are so incredibly fleeting. They do not deserve our servitude. Instead of blind reaction, we must choose empowered action. These reactions were created by continuous repetition and likewise must be destroyed through the continuous repetition of constant awareness.

Never be discouraged by a reaction, for this, in itself, is a reaction. Some reactions are small and only at the surface level of the mind, while others are deep reactions that reflect a karmic choice of fear, repeated over aeons. Any progress is good progress, even if it means you were only angry about something for eight hours when it would have normally taken you nine hours to get over it. Awareness is but one side of the coin, and we must equally develop acceptance.

Acceptance

The first aspect of acceptance is the awareness that we are creating our reality, whether consciously or unconsciously. Whether we believe this literally or not does not change the fact that our experiences are completely directed by our perceptions, values, ideas, and beliefs. We cannot progress without acknowledging this first. The idea is obviously to create consciously. The second aspect of acceptance can be summed up in my guru's mantra: "Everything is perfect and as it should be." Everything in the external world that appears to be happening to us is the result of our internal world and a reflection of the voice we choose to hear. We reap what we sow. Spirit is constantly working amidst our creations, directing us to shed our illusions. If the lessons keep reappearing in different forms, then they have not been learnt. Spirit is always finding ways to direct our growth and lead us to happiness, although we often don't recognise it because we have our own strange ideas and expectations about what we *think* we want.

To truly live with this mantra, we must accept the present moment, including our physical, mental, and emotional self. While we are observing our breath and sensation, we should equally be accepting their present state, with the awareness that all things in this world, including our physical, mental, and emotional self, are impermanent and in a constant state of flux. The bad feelings will pass, just as the good ones will, until all that remains is the love, peace, and joy of God, which is not of this world. It is eternal.

Acceptance is eventually transformed into gratitude. The more we weaken our tendency to react through our past conditioning and strengthen our ability to perceive through spirit, who lives in the present moment, the closer we come to complete gratitude. In this state, everything is possible, for there is no perceived lack. We are full. In this state of fullness, it is impossible not to feel completely grateful, regardless of one's circumstances.

We can now see that our happiness rests in the permanent and not the temporary. It is found in eternity, not in time. It is found in love, not in fear. If we keep basing our happiness on the things of this world, we will always be disappointed, for all the things of the world will soon be dust. A holy man a friend of mine had the pleasure of spending time with in India would refer to this problem as "the God-shaped hole." There is only one thing that will ever fit the shape of our seemingly infinite and insatiable longing. That is divine love.

Meditations and Practices

When you wake every morning, there should be a moment of meditation to observe and remain neutral to your breath, the sensations throughout your entire body, your thoughts, and your emotions. You should also take a moment to reflect on divine love and consciously give your day to divine love. You should also meditate like this just before sleep, with the added task of reflecting on your day. Did you give it to the ego or to spirit?

As much as is possible, it is important to also cultivate these moments in your waking life, with open-eyed meditations as you're going about your day. Observe your breathing, feel the sensations throughout your body, feel the wind through your hair, feel the water on your skin when washing, feel the tools in your hand while working, feel the sun upon your face.

Never allow meditation to feel like a burden. This is the moment you consciously decide for peace. It can take as little as five minutes if you don't have much time; otherwise, you can sit for ten or twenty minutes or even an hour, if you feel comfortable. Always stop when you begin resisting the meditation. I find it helpful to sit cross-legged, as I feel more alert, but always go with what you feel. The following is a simple guide for the objective observation of breath, sensation, thought, and emotion, but this is not set in stone. Meditation is personal and intuitive. Let spirit guide the experience for you.

Meditation

With eyes closed, observe your thoughts and emotions as though you are on the outside, looking in. Do not identify yourself in the thoughts and emotions, for they are not who you are. After observing them for a short time, hand your thoughts and emotions over to spirit. Consciously surrender your thoughts and emotions to a higher power. You can use an affirmation for this or even visualise something that symbolises divine love for you, whether it is Jesus, the Buddha, a white dove, or simply a pure white light.

The thoughts and emotions will likely remain in the beginning, but the total focus on your respiration will quickly become your anchor into the present moment, which is where spirit resides. Relax your entire body from head to feet, breathe through your nose if possible, and place all your attention on your breathing. Do not alter your breathing; just allow it to be as it is, whether shallow or deep. Be intensely focused on each breath in and each breath out, and empty your mind.

Make sure your entire body is still completely relaxed, and place all your attention on the sensations throughout your entire body, from the top of your head to your toes. You may feel many different things, from the obvious sensations that are a result of your environment and sitting for an extended period, to the more subtle sensations throughout your body. It doesn't matter what sensation you feel. What is most important is that you remain calm, neutral, and objective about these sensations. Allow them to be as they are, and do not react to them. Do not resist negative sensations like pain, and do not develop attachment to any pleasant sensations. Simply observe your sensations in a state of utter acceptance and surrender.

Now come back to your symbol for divine love, and sit in the light for a time. Sit in peace. Know that you are eternal, know that you are supported always, know that you are infinitely and eternally loved, and know that you *are* love. Be grateful for this love. Find other things to be grateful for. Now feel the need for all beings to know this love. May all beings know love. Feel the entire earth being bathed in the light of infinite and eternal love. If it is your morning meditation, consciously give the day to divine love. My favourite affirmation for this is from *A Course in Miracles*: "This day I give to you." Be you in charge, for I would follow you, certain that your direction gives me peace. I personally add two other affirmations: May I hear only your voice, and may I share only your love. Make your affirmations personal and relevant to your journey. If it is night, ask that your communication with spirit remain, even in sleep.

A Universal Curriculum

We are all learning the same curriculum in infinite forms. Stated most simply, every moment presents us with only two choices: fear or love. May we all choose wisely.

EGO	SPIRIT
Fear	Love
Anxiety	Peace
Depression	Joy
Judgement	Compassion
Reaction	Action
Control	Surrender
Desire	Gratitude
Resistance	Acceptance
Unconsciousness	Awareness
Time	Eternity
Past and future	Present
Scarcity	Abundance
Illness	Health
Distraction	Concentration
Anger	Serenity
Attack	Healing
Defence	Openness
Doubt	Trust
Confusion	Clarity
Frustration	Patience
Heaviness	Lightness
Struggle	Flow
Meaninglessness	Purpose
Selfishness	Service
Guilt	Forgiveness
Death	Life
Emptiness	Fullness

Thoughts from My Heart after Being Baptised for a Third Time

Submerged in water, arising,
The Spirit descended on me like a dove.
It's true I felt the peace of God,
Surrounded in unconditional love.

Heavy hands holding me down,
Releasing the evil that isn't mine.
The silence under water spoke so loudly,
Each and every part of me divine.

Time stood still as I was lifted,
Cleansed for all to see,
Suspense echoed as to who would arise.
My heart full, knowing I was still me.

I was still me.

Printed in the United States
By Bookmasters